The idea of a world university

THE IDEA OF A

WORLD UNIVERSITY

MICHAEL ZWEIG

Edited with a foreword by **Harold Taylor**

Southern Illinois University Press
Carbondale and Edwardsville

Feffer & Simons, Inc.
London and Amsterdam

FOREWORD

FOUR YEARS ago, at the invitation of the late William Heard
Kilpatrick and a group of his colleagues who had formed a
Committee for the Promotion of an International University in
America, I began a study of the idea of a world university and
the problems connected with establishing such an institution in
the United States or elsewhere. I had become convinced over the
years, partly through my work at Sarah Lawrence College and
the free and easy association we had there with members of the
United Nations delegations and secretariat, that the world community of intellectuals badly needed an institutional base quite
different from any now available. It would be a place where the
world's variety of national cultures, ideologies and forms of
knowledge could be brought together in a new kind of center—a
world university which would match on an intellectual scale

what the United Nations was designed to accomplish in a political dimension.

The argument is a simple one. The scholar and the intellectual owe their allegiance to the ideal of full intellectual inquiry and exchange among all men in all fields of knowledge. Yet national systems of university education limit by their nature the possibility of such inquiry and make demands for allegiance to certain local values and truths which are assumed rather than explored. The lack of opportunity for the continual confrontation of these varieties of truth with each other has meant the consolidation of intellectual blocs which roughly parallel the political blocs now in existence between East and West, North and South. Certain inroads have of course been made—through international congresses of scholars, the Pugwash meetings between Eastern and Western scientists, the increase of exchanges between students and scholars of the seven continents, the work of UNESCO, the International Geophysical Year, and the internationalizing of trade and transportation. Ours is a world of nationalisms continually forced into internationalisms of one sort or another. But full recognition of the necessities and possibilities of internationalism in cultural and intellectual affairs has lagged behind the facts of the world situation, and the world's educational system is presently in danger of becoming less, rather than more, internationalized as the political divisions and antagonisms multiply and coalesce into institutional forms.

At the beginning of my study, I had not realized how often and with what enthusiasm proposals for world universities and international education centers had been made in recent years. A rough estimate would be that since the end of World War I, more than one thousand such proposals have been made, some by private individuals, mainly in Western countries, others by international bodies of scholars and professionals, occasionally by government representatives. As Michael Zweig points out in the present volume, one of the first proposals made to the League of Nations after its founding was for a fully international university to be sponsored by the League, staffed by a completely international faculty and attended by an international student body. Mr. Zweig has done a great service to the field of education by providing a brief history and analysis of the rationale of the world university, beginning with the growth of internationalism following World War I and extending to recent proposals and experiments of the 1950's and 1960's.

Mr. Zweig's interest in the subject comes from his work as a student at the University of Michigan with a student-faculty committee entitled Association for Commitment to World Responsibility. In its beginning, the Association took on the task of drawing up a prospectus for a Peace Corps, and followed that by study and research on the establishment of a United Nations University. Mr. Zweig became interested in the variety of plans which other groups, including the Kilpatrick Committee, had been making for institutions similar to the Michigan version of the United Nations University. In pursuit of further information about such plans and their history, Mr. Zweig spent six months travelling and studying in Europe, particularly in Geneva, Brussels, and Paris, where he reviewed library materials and, at UNESCO in Paris, conferred with officials and consulted the original documents available in the UNESCO archives.

It has been my privilege to review and edit Mr. Zweig's manuscript, to add examples and suggestions from my own experience and research and, with the aid of Shuhud Sa'id, a Malayan student from the World College pilot project described by Mr. Zweig later in the present book, to compile a general summary of world university projects and proposals of the past twenty-five years. Persons who are interested in pursuing the subject of world education further will find in that summary some interesting and important examples. They range from institutions which in some ways approach the ideal of pure internationalism in education to others which are international in the sense that a number of countries are represented in the research staff, the faculty, the student body, and the curriculum.

Among those most directly related to the United Nations, two institutions deserve special mention. The first is the United

Nations International School in New York City where children from sixty-eight countries attend classes from kindergarten to the end of high school and are taught by a faculty representing eighteen countries. The children are sons and daughters of members of the UN Secretariat and Delegations, along with American children from New York. The curriculum is broadly based and involves world conceptions. The final three years of pre-university education are devoted to tutorial preparation of students for admission to their home universities. With a Board of Trustees consisting of members of the UN Secretariat and Americans, the School is financed by tuition fees and a modest subsidy from the United Nations itself. It is entirely possible that the graduates of the UN School, along with Americans and additional students from abroad, could together form the nucleus of a student body for a United Nations College in New York, whose faculty and curriculum could be completely international.

The other institution is the new United Nations Institute for Training and Research in New York City, established by a United Nations Assembly resolution in 1963, for the training of international diplomats, using the original materials, practical problems, and to some extent the personnel of the United Nations. The Board of Trustees is completely international, as is the student body, and the Institute is supported by contributions from UN member countries, individuals, and private foundations. Were the Institute to evolve a curriculum in the arts, sciences, and humanities in addition to the social and political science program, it might well become a United Nations University. There are already in existence the potential branches of such a university in the institutions organized in various countries by the United Nations and UNESCO for special training in problems of social and economic development.

Or, in another sector of world educational need, it is not too difficult to conceive an international Peace Corps Center where the youth of the world could come together to study the total problem of economic, social, and personal development in all

viii

countries, with a view to learning how to solve the particular problems of particular countries by internationally organized effort. We have only begun to scratch the surface of educational content and methods for the education of American Peace Corps volunteers, yet it has been clear for some time that education designed to develop understanding, skill, and knowledge for the solution of human problems in a culture other than one's own, is of a completely different kind than education designed for academic competence in one's own culture. There is already in existence an organization for work in Peace Corps style on an international scale. It is the International Secretariat for Volunteer Service, with forty-two member countries all of whom have volunteers abroad or at home, or are planning to form such groups. A world center for the training and education of even these forty-two nationalities would be a first step toward a radically different kind of education of infinitely more worth than much of the undergraduate studies now conducted in the world's universities.

One Latin-American writer has described the need of the emerging countries in this way.

> We dream of a school which will mean to the peasant not only a place where his children go to learn to read and write, but the place where he himself will find instruction, advice, and assistance in agriculture, medical knowledge, sanitation methods, suggestions about housing, how to organize community action, find a stimulus to his intellectual curiosity, with folklore groups, cinema, concerts, libraries, workshops, experimental theatre, games. . . .

A world college for the preparation of teachers and educators who could start this kind of school and college in their own countries or elsewhere would perform a service to the entire world. The first task of education is not, as is generally assumed, to teach the subject matter of the arts and sciences. It is to raise the level of awareness and response to *all* ideas, events, people, and objects. If there is a narrow range of possibility in the area of response—a uniformity of ideas, people, objects, events—then the level of awareness remains comparably low, the education itself becomes narrowing in its effects.

The experience of teaching in the world college experiment, described later in this book, was a revelation to me of how confined had been my own previous thinking about education and world affairs. To have the youth of the entire world as pupils, to look at ideas and issues from the point of view not merely of Communists or anti-Communists, but of every kind of political, religious, racial, cultural, and personal difference, meant that teaching itself became an illuminating experience by reason of the breadth of point of view which the pupils made necessary. Nothing less than a world view would encompass their variety, and nothing less than the tolerance of the teacher for all the possible views in the world would suffice as a context for their instruction. The sooner we reconstruct totally our conceptions of what education is and what should be its content, and the sooner we give up the idea that the present Western-centered university curriculum is the ideal structure of knowledge for all mankind, the sooner we can link together the cultures of the world in new forms of international cooperation. In the meantime, the number of persons and organizations interested in new conceptions of world education continues to grow, and it is entirely possible that within the next ten years new institutions of a fully international character may spring up in many parts of the world under the influence of such conceptions.

The enormous possibility in the use of new world histories like the series being developed by UNESCO, the use of television programs transmitted through the international communications satellites, the use of films and radio tapes from a variety of nationalities, joint scientific enterprises and studies designed to aid the developing countries, other studies to develop solutions to political and ideological conflict, the use of new computer technologies for the storage and transmission of knowledge on a world scale—all these must somehow be realized if we are not to waste the contributions which modern science, technology, and scholarship can make to the education and enrichment of the whole world. There is already a large body of experience available from the work of the UN Special Fund, the work in economic and social planning of the UN Economic and Social Council, the joint efforts in the peaceful uses of atomic energy, the international Oceanographic Project in the Indian Ocean to show what can be done through cooperative effort on the part of the world's scholars and scientists. The next step is to make this experience available to the world's students.

It would therefore be greatly to the advantage of every country in the world not only to open up all national universities to a much wider variety of international students, faculty, and curriculum, but to establish in key points on the seven continents new institutions where the conception of the unity of mankind and the essential unity of man's knowledge can find expression in what is taught and what is learned.

Harold Taylor

PREFACE

SINCE THE end of the First World War, individuals and groups around the world have turned their attention to the idea of a World University, an International University, a United Nations University—some sort of supranational institute of higher learning. Initiative in the field has come from such separated places as Brazil, China, Spain, India, Poland, Germany, Colombia, the United States, Japan, and Mexico, among others.

Concern has been expressed by a wide variety of individuals not speaking for any government. As early as 1919 Belgian and French educators Paul Otlet and Henri LaFontaine led a movement to establish an International University in Brussels. They were successful for a time, but lack of funds eventually doomed the University in the mid-thirties. Bertrand Russell wrote in 1942 urging the establishment of an international university.

Addressing an international conference on education in Stockholm in 1962, Dwight Eisenhower spoke explicitly in favor of a world university. Great Britain's Sir Alfred Zimmern, an important contributor to the early planning and development of UNESCO, as well as a member of many education committees of the League of Nations, has written about and worked for the establishment of world centers of scholarship, particularly in the social sciences. Albert Einstein welcomed the idea of international higher education in 1949. Henri Laugier, long an important figure at the Sorbonne and for a time Assistant Secretary-General of the United Nations, has expressed a desire for an international university, especially in Africa. Kenneth Boulding of the University of Michigan has written in the field as has Harold Taylor, former President of Sarah Lawrence College and Director of the pilot project for a World College conducted on Long Island in 1963. The list can be extended to include many others, some of whom will be considered later in this book.

In addition to the backing of individuals around the world and going beyond the plans and programs of groups of students, businessmen, and educators, national governments have also rallied to the effort. As we shall see in detail in the text that follows, the governments of Spain, Mexico, Colombia, Poland, China, and France have all come forth with suggestions for world centers of higher learning. UNESCO itself once expressed interest in the establishment of an international university.

What is contained in these pages is a history and analysis of the proposals and projects formulated toward the end of international higher education. I have begun with an explanation of the history of the idea because it is necessary to understand the various rationales put forth on its behalf in order to reach an accurate appreciation and evaluation of the proposals which have been made. Four chapters of the study are devoted to a description of the proposals themselves. Chapters 3, 4, and 5 deal with each proposal as a whole; the Appendices summarize typical proposals and existing institutions. The past failure of exponents of international higher education to develop sound and practicable solutions to these problems has led to a certain amount of skepticism in many minds as to the feasibility of a world university. The beginning of Chapter 6 sets forth a more complete explanation of the lack of success which has characterized attempts so far to establish an international university. The last part of this chapter takes up in detail some of the issues of practicality which have presented recent difficulties. Partially based on past work, some tentative conclusions are reached on the questions of language, location, and curriculum. In particular, the meaning and feasibility of an international university depends first upon private groups marshalling support from foundations, students, scholars, and other interested persons, and second upon the participation of national governments in some form of international intellectual body.

The word international itself offers special problems in the description of an educational institution. In the sense in which I use it, it describes a situation in which students, faculty, and administration are drawn from the widest possible national and cultural origins, representing most, if not all, of the nations of the world, and certainly all of the political and cultural blocs. But a further qualification must be made, that no single culture, no single ideology, no single point of view obscure any other. This definition of international may turn out to be, strictly applied, barely within practical achievement. While its achievement has been a thorny problem for other so-called international associations, there is nothing inherently impossible or self-contradictory in the definition. This definition of international higher education only suggests that some curriculum exists, but it says nothing ex hypothesi as to its range or content. The range of disciplines studied and the nature of research will vary with the intent of a particular proposal and the financial resources available. While higher education commonly includes all studies at universities or colleges, including undergraduate work as that term is used in the United States, proponents of international higher education have usually envisioned a center of postgraduate and graduate studies.

It should be noted from the outset that this definition of international higher education excludes a great many projects and institutions normally associated with the term. For instance, CERN (European Organization for Nuclear Research) does not fall directly into our purview because it does not offer a full curriculum, even in physics, nor is it freely open to physicists from outside Europe. The College of Europe is equally disqualified because it is not, strictly speaking, a world center of higher education. The same may be said for the several regional education and research centers in Africa, Asia, and Latin America. All are expressions of at least some part of the movement toward higher education of a fully international character. In fact, they are by-products of that movement. This wider definition of international has been set to focus attention more easily on the increasing pressure for international higher education in its pure form, and assumes that other less strictly international units have been the result of that pressure so far. While mention should be made of these semi-international (or local) higher education and research centers, our main interest here will be in the parent movement, the original hope. In this way we will better see precisely what the drive for international higher education includes, and will be able to judge its current significance by comparing the ideal international university with the already existing multinational institutes.

This book is aimed at illuminating the rationale and history of twentieth-century efforts to establish a world university. If it also motivates some to channel their resources and energies in that direction, or if it advances the thinking and activity of those already working in the field, it will have achieved more than its original purpose.

I would like to acknowledge gratefully the assistance of a number of people who have helped enormously in the development of this book and the ideas in it. Were it not for Judy and Julian Gomez and Mrs. Joan Chesler, I would likely never have developed my interest in this field. The research was largely made possible by the financial aid of Mr. William Swartz of Chicago, Illinois. The archival librarians at UNESCO in Paris and the UN in Geneva were splendid in their response to my general inquiries, and produced volumes of relevant material which contained much of the historical information. My wife, Martha, worked patiently to type much of the original manuscript, improving it as she worked, and Dr. Harold Taylor made further important contributions to the final version. I have particularly appreciated the attention and aid given me by Mrs. Violet Lannoy of the UNESCO Department of Education, who encouraged me often during my stay in Paris, and to whom this book is dedicated.

Ann Arbor, Michigan   *Michael Zweig*
April 8, 1966

CONTENTS

The idea of a world university

1

THE NEED FOR A WORLD UNIVERSITY

E A C H P R O P O S A L for a center of international higher education has begun with some statement of need, a justification for interest in the field. In fact, a great many suggestions for international universities have been little more than that. Usually, the details of the university, its administration, and curriculum, have been left to further study. The validity of the idea of international higher education is generally conceded. The major impediment to the establishment of a world university, however, has been the failure of its proponents to come forth with detailed plans. Another crucial block has been the doubt of many that a world university is really the most efficient means of achieving the series of desirable ends.

If we are to understand the proposals of the last four

3

decades, we must recognize and understand the desires which motivated them. If we are to assess the value of this history of plans, we must also try to see their relevance to the desires which prompted them. It is with these two tasks that the present chapter deals. In the most general terms, proposals for a world university have had two broad aims: political and educational. Proponents have developed a wide range of statements within these two categories, but no single author has drawn on all the rationales which we shall discuss here. In total, the politically oriented rationales outnumber the educational ones, but this is not to say that the educative functions of the world university have ever been neglected. On the contrary, its advocates have had deep faith in the role of education in the building of a politically, culturally, and physically compatible, if not homogeneous, world society. If politics is a prime factor in the aims of international higher education, it is so because men have seen a political, or rather a social, need for international education.

In 1925, Professor R. Barany, then director of the Otolaryngological Clinic at the University of Upsala in Sweden, placed before the League of Nations Committee on Intellectual Cooperation a "Scheme for the Establishment of an International University for the Training of Statesmen, Diplomats, Politicians, Political Editors, and Professors in High Schools of Political Science." [1] Barany declared that "this would constitute a highly important factor in raising the level of political conscience in all nations." He prefaced his brief scheme with the observation that "a statesman should be acquainted not only with the interests of his own nation, but also—and to an equal degree—with the interests of the other nations with which his fellow citizens come in contact." [2]

This desire to see national politicians and other politically oriented people imbued with a sense of international context was carried into a number of subsequent proposals and eventually expanded to include the training of interna-

4

tional civil servants. After World War II, with the previous failure of the League of Nations, and with the newly created United Nations dedicated to similar tasks, some concern was expressed that the staff of international political bodies should have an international perspective. In 1952, Alexander Marc, British professor of social science, turned his attention to an international university and included among its tasks the completion of "the training of international leaders who would be able to play an effective part in popular education, in the organization of supra-national movements, institutions and associations, and in cooperation between the different countries, religions, races, etc." [3]

In 1962, the Association for Commitment to World Responsibility (ACWR), a student-faculty organization at the University of Michigan, went still further and declared that "a United Nations University would offer the ideal opportunity for training members of an international police force, an international inspection team, or an international jury." [4]

These three different expressions all point toward the training of international civil servants through the development of political minds which will serve the international community, either from the vantage of an international organization or from a position in a single nation. They all imply the important assertion that this international service is desirable, if not vital; and, conversely, that strict national allegiances and orientations are undesirable, if not dangerous. These implications have found direct expression in various proposals. The aim of developing international orientation is made explicit by Alexander Marc when he writes that the goal of an international university should be to "guide young people, in a truly Federalist spirit, towards an understanding of the major theoretical and practical issues of our time," and further, "to establish a center of information on all questions bearing on 'structural' reforms in different fields, with special reference to the 'federalization' of

5

European and world structures." [5] The proposal now takes on a new direction, viz., toward the eventual federalization of nations.

The desire to form new perspectives and new political orientations is stated succinctly by Eugene Staley, an international economist at the Stanford Research Institute. He says: "In this era of world-ranging weapons and world-wide interplay of ideas, we must expand our sense of citizenship . . . we must add a new dimension of citizenship and loyalty—that to the world community." With a note of urgency he adds, "Unless enough men in enough countries do this soon enough, we may all perish." [6] The Michigan (ACWR) proposal also puts forth a justification for a United Nations University on the grounds that political and social realities of our age require a new approach. "Increasingly, man's relation to his fellow man has come to be an international relationship; yet we have no adequate international training ground to prepare those who must one day bear this burden of negotiating between cultures. A United Nations University is needed as a means of providing the psychological and emotional experience of cultural interaction free of the restrictive demands of national commitment. . . . Armed with this experience the approach to international relations by these students might be able to assume new dimensions." [7]

The impatience with national allegiance and national orientation untempered by a higher international responsibility, of which the desire to train international civil servants is only a symptom, has led to two suggested positive substitutes, both variations on international loyalty. One, exemplified by the ACWR proposal, calls for the eventual elimination of distinct nations in favor of one international world government enjoying the undivided allegiance of all the peoples of the world. A second, milder and more readily received alternative has been an international allegiance to a world federal government, stemming from the United Na-

6

tions, but with the continued lesser allegiance to the individ-ual nations. Staley typifies this approach with the observa-tion that "while remaining good and loyal members of our families, proud and cooperative citizens of our home towns and provinces or states, loyal citizens of our nations, we must add a new dimension of citizenship and loy-alty. . . ." [8] In either case, a world university is seen as an initiator of the desired broader loyalties.

A very strong case can be made that a broadening of national responsibilities is needed. The allegiance of the contemporary citizen is to his own country and, in the last analysis, he is responsible only to it. This is in the very nature of nationalism. Yet the nation itself has allegiances and responsibilities to the rest of the world, organizationally through the United Nations, UNESCO, and other bodies and, less formally, through exchanges, aid programs, and international finance. The nation also has the obligation of avoiding war. But nations are not entities separate from their citizens. They are a reflection of the people in them. A nation can, in the long run, assume only those responsi-bilities and allegiances which its people accept. In the mod-ern world of national loyalties felt by all peoples, nations have ventured slightly forward toward new responsibilities, toward supranational allegiances. If these new international organizations and responsibilities are to become enduring, something must be done to impart to the people a deep feeling for and identification with the new world loyalty undertaken hesitatingly by governments under the enor-mous pressure of the times.

Here we have the full force of the paradox of our age. The people of the world are possessed of little, if any, feeling of international responsibility. Yet the characteristics of the times—the technology which brings us all together, and the revulsion at the thought of war which gives us a common purpose—have led nations into international agreements. The responsibilities of those agreements cannot be fulfilled, except in the most tentative of circumstances, without similar international loyalties felt by the people of each country. It is this paradox which lies at the heart of the proposals for international higher education and their expressed impatience with nationalism. But it must be recognized that such impatience does involve a moral judgment. It holds that popular loyalties should be raised to support international relations, and that mankind cannot afford the risks of war resulting from national myopia unchecked by international responsibilities. The task of developing new supranational popular loyalties is seen by some as an important function of a world university. This analysis of the paradox explains why serious thinking on the matter arose only after the first World War, with the building of the League of Nations; in spite of its failure, the League was a first great step into supranational allegiances forced upon the world by the growing complexity and interrelationships of the age and was directly precipitated by the recognition of the fact that war had become impossible. People began to look for a way to imbue at least the national leaders and potential leaders, if not entire peoples, with the urgency of international responsibility. This is the crux of the political case for international higher education. But to recognize the underlying goal of international higher education as important and desirable is not at once to say that international higher education is the proper means, or even a relevant means, for achieving that goal. I shall return to this question in the next chapter, but I first wish to deal with the educational aims of a world university.

The first proposal for an international university to emerge after World War I was that of Paul Otlet and the Union of International Associations, formed privately in 1919 to promote international cooperation in educational and cultural affairs. Mr. Otlet and his group developed a program based in part on the need for advanced studies of international social science problems. Alexander Marc quotes Otlet as saying, "The first and general aim of the university will be to ensure that the teaching provided makes a systematic contribution toward synthesizing and classifying branches of knowledge, recording their history, improving their methods, and defining their more general problems and results." [9] Speaking in 1925, Otlet explained that "the development of international life, of science and educations, of method and efficiency with regard to theory and practice . . . emphatically urge upon us the necessity of establishing a world university," and that the university "should endeavor to imbue scientific research with the spirit of synthesis and correlation." [10]

But the development of new synthesis and methods in the social and natural sciences was not the only goal of Otlet's Brussels International University. He also saw it as a central ground from which students from around the world would take home common experience and some common background. He described it also as a "University of the universities," coordinating and initiating research and exchange programs and developing an international library and reference center. It was to be an "institute where the principles of universal civilization and the doctrine of the League of Nations will be elaborated and presented." In this regard he is close to expressing a desire for supranational loyalties, suggesting that "An international university would be the best laboratory for producing the general doctrine needed by the League of Nations, the best vehicle for the principles of universal civilization . . . the best method for generating a kind of central impulse for the intellectual life of all Humanity. Better than any administrative organization, it would be able to coordinate thought, harmonize acts, and prepare the future." [11] Otlet's work remains to this day one of the most comprehensive visions of international higher education, anticipating and combining many points to be made later by others.

In 1951 the International Association of University Professors and Lecturers (IAUPL) described another source of interest in a world university, particularly in relation to the social sciences. Presenting the IAUPL position, British professors T. S. Simey and F. T. H. Fletcher note that it is a "fallacy . . . to suppose that the work carried out by national institutions can ultimately be relied upon to solve international problems by a kind of automatic process . . . [for] such projects as the study of barriers to communication at international conferences . . . it is extremely unlikely that such problems can be tackled effectively with tools borrowed, as it were, from the stock created for other purposes, such as market research, the treatment of delinquency or the maintenance of industrial morale. All the techniques so far employed are relevant in some degree, as they are designed to assist the processes of changing human behavior; where the importance of solving international problems, however, is of such a high order that the very future of our race may depend upon it, the conclusion can only be that special skills and techniques must be invented." [12]

The IAUPL looks to an international social science institute to develop the new methods and analyses to cope with modern international political relations. They see the first task of the institute to be the creation of "an informed body of opinion . . . as to the need to carry out the work. . . . Its second task will be to educate young social scientists in the realities of the problems of international relations and the methods which experience has proved most effective to deal with them." Once the needs have been determined and all present methods fully understood, the full resources of the social scientists of the entire world could be brought to bear on "a fully developed research program."

The IAUPL details more fully Otlet's original desire to see new approaches created for the study of social problems. There is also a specific concern for studies of barriers to communication at international conferences. More recently, the Association for Commitment to World Responsibility (ACWR) has also suggested that a United Nations University might study problems of communication, but the question was put into a larger context and represents still another goal of international higher education—the study of conflict and conflict resolution when cultures and/or ideologies collide. The ACWR proposal points out that wars and other serious international disruptions develop when international relations, expressed in terms of mutual image, fear and reaction among nations, break down under political tensions caused by cultural or ideological confrontations. Their proposal asserts that it would be a valuable contribution to peace if the exact nature of political tension could be defined and, further, if the mechanisms were known by which confrontation spawns resentment, tension, and eventual open conflict. If this were known, we could perhaps prevent the development of open conflict by avoiding the initial stages. ACWR sees a United Nations University as the logically perfect place to study these problems.

The desire to give people of all nations some degree of common experience has also prompted proposals for international higher education. Otlet writes, "In this Center of High Culture students from all countries will live together and have a common life. Tomorrow these students will everywhere be at the head of business, education, science, administration and politics. They will learn to know and respect one another and will form close personal relationships for the rest of their lives." Otlet wanted all students at his university to spend six months together traveling around the world on an academic tour. He hoped that ten years' operation would generate "a chosen group of five thousand to ten thousand young people having seen the world and having a real understanding of its major problems." [13]

For similar reasons the government of China proposed to the UNESCO preparatory commission in 1946 that UNESCO establish a series of United Nations Universities, one in each continent. "Their purpose would be to gather men and women from different countries to give them a common life and a common aim in pursuing the higher knowledge." [14]

The ACWR proposal suggests another advantage of assembling representatives of many cultures and ideologies at an international university. It points out that a United Nations University could "contribute to the establishment of peace by clarifying the concept of peace and what it involves . . . through its educational and social curricula." This touches on another important goal of international higher education, the development and propagation of uniform definitions of social and political terms in the effort to reduce difficulties of communication. It goes beyond uniform understanding of the word "peace."

Just as there is an international Bureau of Weights and Measures to standardize definitions around the world, so there might well be advances made toward the standardization of terms used in political and economic measurement and description. The chaos of measuring international trade without standardized quantitative units has been partially set in order by international recognition of certain definitions. The chaos of international politics has yet to be ordered, and an important step would surely be a standardization of the quantitative and qualitative terms used in political analyses. Such everyday terms as "peace," "freedom," "slavery," "socialism," "conflict," all need careful definitions which will be common to academic and political circles in the many nations. If the nations of the world are to work together for the establishment and maintenance of a situation called peace, it is imperative that at some early date in that work the nations come to some general agreement as to the substance of their aim. Otherwise, quite obviously, combined effort will be impossible since all parties will not be addressing the same problem. If common effort is to be achieved and carried through, points of similarity of aim, i.e., definition, must be found, structured and expressed.

12

This observation applies not only to cooperative peace offensives, but also to international social and economic development programs and, in fact, to every other international effort which is defined by words.

If all of the goals of international higher education described so far have had some political roots, there have also been purely academic advantages attributed to a world university. As we have seen, Paul Otlet included in his list of objectives the synthesis and coordination of academic research in all fields. He described the international university as the logical and necessary sequel to the founding of single-discipline international academic societies and research laboratories. He felt that the separate works of the many disciplines could be made more efficient and reach new heights if carried out together, facilitating communication, pooled resources, and understanding of progress.

Greatly influenced by Otlet, Alexander Marc also includes academic coordination among his hopes, and holds that an international university "should facilitate the systematic comparison of achievements, and above all of methods, whose significance may be distorted or, . . . whose effectiveness may be impaired by specialization and, . . . by isolationism." [15] He writes that an international university could "establish the closest possible contact with the different university, inter-university and cultural movements, so as to pave the way for effective collaboration in the following fields: regular exchanges of information; co-ordination of programs; inter-change of professors and students; joint organization of study courses and various other activities; gradual establishment of a true World Co-ordination Center." [16]

In this regard, the Rumanian National Committee to the League of Nations suggested in 1923 that an international university would be an "excellent step in the direction of intellectual co-operation." The Greek National Committee proposed that "an international university would greatly help toward the organization of mutual intellectual assistance and, in particular, toward the exchange of professors and students, intellectual co-operation and the work of an international bibliography." [17]

The ACWR proposal lists among its objectives for a United Nations University: "information gathering, appraisal and distribution; world-wide studies like the International Geophysical Year; establishment of an international library where world publications would be collected and transformed into meaningful communications between the nations. . . . It should perhaps house the single greatest translation and redistribution center the world has ever known."

In 1945, the government of Colombia proposed that "UNESCO establish . . . a University of the United Nations, the essential function of which would be to encourage scientific research and higher technical education, but including also other branches of human knowledge." [18] This is one of many similar expressions concerned with an international center of research.

There remains one more major objective which has stimulated interest in international higher education. As expressed by Alexander Marc, "We must think over again the concrete problems facing mankind, in the light of our common destiny. It is the implicit duty of an international university to make this effort to arrive at a restatement, a self-transcendence, a 'revision of all values,' an inventory and a fresh discovery." Eugene Staley has commented that the United Nations University "should dedicate its efforts particularly to the discovery and development of unifying elements in the values widely held by the world's different peoples and cultural traditions."

A UNESCO seminar on education for the development of international understanding observed that "an effective instrument must be set up in the near future for making the people of the various nations aware of their common destiny . . . it must also, above all, encourage the growth of a new mental attitude, without which there can be no international understanding." [19] In the words of Kenneth Boulding, "The world is in desperate need of a symbol of unity and knowledge which transcends all diversity of interest and belief. . . . A United Nations University could be a more vivid symbol and a way of translating the symbol into reality." [20]

This is perhaps the most lofty of all interests, for it seeks to establish a symbol of the common objective and responsibility of all men—serious, peaceful and zealous—searching for the answers to world problems and world questions. It is the responsibility of all men to work together to seek understanding of the world, its conflicts and its unifying points. It is the responsibility of all men to work together to find resolution of our differences. It is the responsibility of all men to work together to understand the causes of poverty and disease and to develop progressive solutions to the problems facing all nations. It is the responsibility of all men to abandon purely nationalist orientation. It is the responsibility of all men to work together toward a world community of shared scientific knowledge and philosophic propositions not delivered at the hands of national jealousies and hatred.

These obligations are not to be achieved by political programs. Rather, their successful execution lies in the development of a new attitude and orientation of men, who must become international in their sense of devotion. The realization of these responsibilities will come about only when men can channel their newly directed devotion into academic study and research. The symbol of that attitude and the locus of that study can be only an international university.

These, then, are the several goals ascribed to international higher education. They include the training of international civil servants and the generation of international loyalties and sympathies. They include coordination and synthesis of research, academic communication and exchanges, and the study of international conflict resolution. Men have hoped to institutionalize opportunities for multinational contact and confrontation. Men have sought better international understanding through the discovery or development of common definitions and new approaches to social and economic problems.

All of these objectives fall under two large and overpowering desires—the development of international understanding, awareness and loyalty to support the first probing steps taken by national governments into international dependence; and the creation of a symbol, constantly present and recognized, to epitomize and demonstrate the unified search for answers to the conflicts and questions of all mankind, requiring the systematic, efficient, simultaneous and dedicated application of men everywhere. These goals have been sympathetically received wherever they have been expressed. In more sophisticated discussions, they are quickly passed over as clear and granted. Men have seemed to want to concentrate, recently, on practical problems, and while those considerations are extremely fundamental and long overdue, there is danger that we lose sight of the ideals motivating us. Once that happens, or once those ideals become fogged and inarticulate, the much needed practical discussion loses its basis, inspiration and orientation.

Now that the goals of international higher education have been described, I wish to turn to two crucial and difficult considerations: the question of possible alternative means of achieving these high aims and the reasons for believing that international higher education is in itself relevant to the attainment of the ends ascribed to it. It is significant that these two points have never been systematically and seriously probed by advocates of international higher education. The omission has allowed a certain skepticism to arise concerning the relevance and applicability of a world university, and UNESCO and the League of Nations have preferred to depend upon bolstering existing institutions.

It is not entirely out of disinterested intellectual curiosity that these questions become important in our consideration of international higher education. Rather, the whole case for and against it rests squarely on the outcome of this investigation because, if existing institutions or some organization more easly attainable than an international university can satisfy our desires, talk of international higher education becomes redundant at best. But even if existing institutions cannot satisfy us we must still prove the relevance of a world university, for it may be that existing institutions and international higher education both fall short of the requisite needs, in which case the vehicle for our satisfaction lies outside the realm of education.

2 THE DEVELOPED ALTERNATIVES

TO A WORLD UNIVERSITY

IT WOULD be misleading to assert or to believe that the goals just described have been neglected in the past forty years, or that only meager effort has been expended to make those dreams real. In fact, large numbers of educational programs have been developed as alternatives to international higher education in the hope that the desired goals be attained.

These alternative programs and institutions fall into five general categories: international exchanges of publications; international exchanges of students and faculty; centers for the study of international relations and the development of area study programs at existing national universities; international academic associations; and UNESCO-sponsored seminars, conferences, and projects such as the Associated Schools Project in Education for International

Understanding and Cooperation. It is to these suggested alternatives that we now turn our attention. Because each one of these approaches is exemplified by large numbers of specific examples, it will be necessary to consider only the general characteristics of each approach in this discussion. We need only ask to what extent each approach can be expected, in principle, to further the goals we have in mind.

Without going into the history of these alternatives, and without analyzing deeply the mechanisms by which each operates, certain of our goals can be related to each, although each may have other objectives. For instance, it might be hoped that the various international academic associations, such as the International Association of Economists, etc., would coordinate research and eliminate duplication of effort, at least in non-classified areas. One might expect that student exchange programs would develop international understanding and offer the common experience which Otlet desired. Existing national universities have been entrusted by UNESCO and the League of Nations with the task of developing feelings of international responsibilities while carrying out advanced social science research on international problems. More recently in the United States, some universities have housed centers for the study of conflict resolution. Faculty exchanges have been used to keep cross-cultural expression flowing, and exchanges of publications have served to distribute new information worldwide. Finally, UNESCO has worked to coordinate educational programs for international understanding and has held numerous conferences of experts to discuss international cultural relations in an academic atmosphere. All of these activities are of value to international understanding and cooperation and may be important for still other reasons. But they remain inadequate as the means of reaching the goals of truly international education.

Exchanges of students and faculty members are rarely more than trilateral, and almost never constitute an opportunity for a flow of ideas from all culture blocs. Exchange programs seldom maintain continuity of cross-cultural exposure, there being no central, permanent international staff at any national university. Almost never, and never by plan, does one find a multinational group of students being taught by an exponent of a culture other than that prevailing in the university country. Further, at the present time, exchange programs tend to put students and faculty from self-proclaimed neutral countries at some disadvantage, since they must go to one of the two political power blocs for advanced studies in many fields. The not uncommon result is the political identification of the individual with the country and bloc in which he studied. In this way, the student or professor, often unjustly tainted, is at a disadvantage when he returns to his own country. Exchanges between the two blocs are themselves infrequent, and participants are characteristically guarded in their expression and receptiveness of "enemy" ideas. While these negative circumstances are not inherent in an exchange program, they are inherent in any such program carried out in this time. The very cold war which gives such urgency to the purposes of international higher education at the same time helps to render the exchange program ineffective as a viable substitute for a world university. These structural characteristics of student and faculty exchange programs limit them from producing the kind of international atmosphere and total confrontation which underlie the objectives of international understanding. Such programs are irrelevant to other goals, especially the creation of a symbol of academic internationalism.

However, exchange programs comprise only one part of the modern national university's attempt to foster and study the betterment of international relations. If the presence on campus of foreign publications, students, and a few professors is not enough to achieve the aims of international higher education, departments of international studies and area-study programs are blossoming. These programs are highly favored by UNESCO and their value in exposing students to new systems of thought should not be minimized. Indeed, such programs are important in developing a balanced exposure to problems and systems of analysis.

Despite the obvious contributions of many distinguished national universities to the field of international studies, and despite the scholarly objectivity which exists at these universities in the presentation of material related to international relations, a number of subtle imbalances and limitations are inherent in national education itself. These limitations make it impossible for a national institution to duplicate the work and atmosphere which could be generated at an international university. Through the staff and curriculum of a world university, students and faculty alike would confront one another with rival ideologies, hypotheses, perspectives, priorities, and attitudes. This confrontation, essential to the nature of international education and to the successful development of international empathies, cannot be matched at a national university where, by definition, the national culture and its presuppositions dominate the intellectual atmosphere.

The fundamentally unilateral nature of the traditional university affords easy escape from whatever limited conflict is produced through exchanges, allowing easy acceptance of the dominant views. This escape is especially open to the adherents of the local beliefs, but is also tempting for the dissenter, newly arrived from another country, guest at his new university, and greatly outnumbered. A more frequent outcome for the foreign student than acquiescence to the majority values is his withdrawal from the community whenever possible. This, of course, stifles the very cross-cultural contact which is to be engendered by the exchange. At an international institution, no single element would dominate; no ideology or value system would limit the terms of the confrontation.

A more critical difficulty related to national education is

the rarity of full expression given to hostile doctrines * at traditional universities. This difficulty is a natural extension of one of the basic and often implicit goals of traditional education, the transmission of a system of values considered fundamental to the society. While this passing of values between generations is vital to the peaceful and steady evolution of individual cultures, it is an automatic barrier to the introduction and full exploration of radically dissenting ideologies which, it is felt, might infect the new generation if dynamically presented at the national universities. This concern for continuity, molding the orientation of private institutions and often explicit within governmentally operated educational systems, limits the opportunity for exploration of doctrines openly hostile to the nation or culture in which the traditional university operates. Because they are less threatening, foreign ideas are not restricted as severely, and in better universities not at all, so that the fundamental conflict arises mainly with regard to hostile beliefs. The conflict cannot be avoided unless the basic objective of traditional education changes.

In the United States, for example, Tufts University and Harvard University have jointly administered the Fletcher School of Law and Diplomacy, a graduate school of international affairs, since 1933. This school offers advanced training in international law, economics, and diplomatic history and is considered one of the better graduate centers in the field. Its aim is the presentation of "a broad program of professional education in international affairs to a select group of graduate students."[1] The curriculum is designed to provide a background for work in "the United Nations and other international agencies, and in international busi-

* Hostile as distinct from foreign. A foreign doctrine is simply one which differs from the culture or beliefs prevalent at the university. A hostile doctrine, on the other hand, is one which is thought to constitute an active threat to the dominant culture. Taoism is a foreign doctrine in the United States, but communism is a hostile one. Catholicism is an hostile doctrine in the Soviet Union, as were Mendelian theories of genetics before Lysenko fell from authority.

ness and journalism," as well as in the United States diplomatic corps.

The student body numbers about one hundred and fifty, including "a number of foreign students as part of an established policy of forming a student body of wide and varied backgrounds." In fact, in 1963, fourteen nations outside the United States [2] were represented by some twenty students. The faculty includes visiting lecturers from the United Nations, also for the purpose of international balance.

Yet the influence of United States policy is evident even in the catalogue. For example, the student training at Fletcher for international service through the United Nations would take Economics 5A, Comparative Economic Systems. According to the catalogue, this is "a comparison of the main contemporary economic systems (capitalism, socialism, *totalitarianism*) as exemplified by the economic structure of different countries (United States, United Kingdom, *U.S.S.R.*)." [3] This use of the word totalitarianism to refer to an economic system instead of a political system is actually an extension of Western-bloc standards into the very definition of the curriculum. The student might enroll in Diplomacy 10A, Latin American Institutions and Inter-American Affairs, where "particular emphasis will be given to certain problems raised by . . . Cuba and Castro and the Sino-Soviet *threat*." Course descriptions include repeated mention of "Communist motives and strategies" contrasted with "United States policy responses," another implied predisposition against the East.[4] Fletcher is not a government-operated school, yet it involves commitment to United States values and policies. The statement of purpose and plan itself suggests as much by declaring that "full recognition" should be given to the "global character of American foreign policy." [5] Incontestably, the student of international relations seeking a clear and balanced study of different approaches to international problems will not be satisfied at Fletcher and similar institutions.

It is true that international curricula at national universities can give students a picture of world problems and present factual information about other outlooks. But at best that picture cannot convey the full depth and color of the realities of international relations. It is like trying to understand the nature and atmosphere of an intricate, delicate, vast and multicolored landscape from an ordinary snapshot. The photograph gives some inkling, and is certainly better than nothing, but in no sense can it be considered equal to the actual experience. Similarly, the understanding and appreciation of various national attitudes and international relations and problems can be taught only in an atmosphere of confrontation equal to that of the real world. No national university has yet been able to offer this kind of atmosphere.

Besides considerations of education for international understanding, a national university is incompatible with the goals of international higher education in other ways. No national university would have the time or motivation to act as a central coordinator of research in different fields; nor would any single national institution be acceptable to all nations and universities as a liaison among individuals and institutions. Further, the fact that the university is identified with a single nation makes it impossible to be recognized as an international academic symbol, limiting its value as a research center of UNESCO, the United Nations, and other international organizations which might be able to come to more rapid, more effective conclusions of international social problems by referring those problems to an academic staff.

UNESCO, however, has centered its educational programs for international understanding and cooperation on the national education systems, with increased emphasis in recent years on primary and secondary school education. One important UNESCO project in this area has been the UNESCO Associated Schools Project in Education for International Understanding and Cooperation. The program, directed at secondary schools in different countries, was to encourage "comprehensive projects of experimental

24

activities designed to increase knowledge of world affairs and international understanding, with emphasis on the aims and work of the United Nations and its specialized agencies, and on the principles of the Universal Declaration of Human Rights." By 1957, over one hundred schools in thirty-two countries were offering children two- to six-week courses consistent with the purpose of the program. UNESCO made literature available and encouraged national systems to adopt the plan.

The Associated Schools Project typifies the type of direction which UNESCO gives, preferring to suggest and promote activity by national school systems themselves. Detailing the results of the Project presented problems, as reported by UNESCO in 1958.[6] "Significance of the findings obtained is restricted in many instances by the imprecision of criteria and the inadequacy of research designs and facilities for research." As it presently operates, UNESCO does not have the time or money systematically and deeply to assess the results of its numerous conferences, seminars, and programs, and therein lies one of its weaknesses.

Elton B. McNeil has discussed the "extreme difficulty of overcoming the nationalism" which dominates students in their approach to studying international relations. McNeil writes that "Dr. Charles A. McClelland at San Francisco State College participated in one such three year study designed to make international relations less remote to the average American student, and he reported himself to be shaken by the outcome. Choosing for study specific world areas such as the Far East, he discovered that a compulsory course was not able to teach students to think more critically or effectively or even to acquire more information about international relations. If anything, the student response revealed that the effort had generated a high degree of distrust of the professor, the specially prepared text book, and of the institution itself. . . . Some students felt it was an effort to brainwash or manipulate them. . . . In light of the outcome of this recent attempt to educate students about their international attitudes and beliefs, it becomes clear that the task of international education will be an herculean one." [7]

What is also clear is that the effort should be carried out in as international an environment as possible, as divorced from any dominant political orientation as possible. The problem is broader than political inquiry, affecting scientific, artistic, and philosophic discussion, all of which need unprejudiced atmosphere for exploration. National universities at the present time are unable to meet this requirement.

The major difficulty with UNESCO efforts is that they are channeled to national educational institutions, where the pressures and limitations discussed above take effect. The one type of activity carried on by UNESCO and other international organizations, academic and governmental, which can overcome these imbalances is the international seminar. At such meetings scholars and experts from around the world exchange ideas and experience and try to work out solutions to common problems. The main difficulty with these seminars is their short duration and the lack of opportunity to study deeply any of their results, even the most tentative. There are large numbers of conferences and meetings, but rarely are the results compared and/or synthesized.

The activities of international academic associations are valuable in eliminating duplication of effort and disseminating new information. Beyond professional journals, their international conferences and conventions do afford the opportunity for short-lived deep intellectual confrontation and offer some coordination of research. But, as presently constituted, international academic associations cannot satisfy our goals, mainly because the international meetings are so few and so short. In addition, these associations are not in any way oriented toward or open to the student, so that their direct value in the educational process is reduced.

Recognizing that an international academic association,

meeting only occasionally, had neither the time nor the facilities to carry out constructive and collaborative research, UNESCO and other international organizations developed the European Organization for Nuclear Research, (CERN), designed to draw the finest minds in physics to facilities unsurpassed in Europe. There they were to work together on problems wherever possible and share experience and method. Some excellent work is being done, with a small permanent international staff and a resident program. It is open primarily to Europeans, although a small number of non-European physicists are received. This program is close to the research facilities needed for our purposes, but to be fully international it should be less dominated by Europe and should include research centers for many more branches of learning. Even so expanded, it would need a larger teaching program for students before it could assume the full scope of an international university.

This cursory look at the alternatives to international higher education is not meant to provide a balanced analysis of all their aspects. But the considerations raised are enough to show that none of the programs can adequately meet the goals of a world university, however many other tasks they can and do perform. The lack of personal collaboration and debate can be overcome by personal exchanges, but the national atmosphere of the university cannot be escaped; nor does the conservative nature of the national educational system allow the free interchange one finds at a meeting of representatives of many cultures. National universities give way to a University of Europe, and CERN is developed to expand contact and internationalize facilities. Each step comes closer to affording solutions to our problems, but so far none is appropriate. The direction is certainly toward an international university in our original strict sense of the term.

If it is now evident that the alternatives to international higher education cannot meet the needs, we must look for positive reasons to believe that a world university could serve as an effective means to our ends. Just as in the above discussion, we will be limited to expectations arising from definition, and will ask if there is anything inherent in the concept of a world university contrary to our goals. Some of the practical problems of instituting any idealized program will be dealt with in Chapter 6. Since there presently exists no international university which can serve as a model,[8] let us construct one on paper with no thought as yet to practicability.

Let us suppose a full-scale university of five thousand students, large faculty, excellent laboratory, library, and research facilities, offering doctorates in many disciplines in the humanities, social and natural sciences. Suppose further that the students come from over one hundred and twenty countries and are distributed according to our strict definition of international, as given in the Preface. Assume the same distribution for the faculty and administration. Let the fully accredited university be located in Geneva, and assume that the average student completes his studies there in three to four years. Of course all students, faculty and administrators are from among the best of their home countries. What reason is there to believe that such a university could substantively contribute to the many aims ascribed to it?

To speak first of the educational goals, this hypothetical world university would engender constant confrontation of ideas. Discussion and definition of political, social, and philosophical terms might be a specialized case. The university would allow the freest and most fundamental discussion and probing since it would, as an institution, be dedicated or responsible to no single orientation or ideology.

Research of all kinds would find extended collaboration, and with normal channels of communications open to national universities, a coordinated, nonduplicative research program could be effected, including cooperation impossible under any present system. This research might take the

28

form of continued International-Geophysical-Year-type activity, or the faculty could study the results of pilot projects and conferences which today remain only hastily summarized.

The international university would not put an end to political and social differences, but those differences would at least be presented in the critical sphere of academics rather than through the polemical claims of politics and propaganda machines. Since the university would be a scaled-down model of the intellectual world as a whole, it would be an excellent place to study barriers to communication among different cultures. Conflict studies could also be conducted. Both might be more successfully carried out at a world university since the intellectual atmosphere there would be a closer approximation to the real international situation than that of a national university.

Placed in such an international atmosphere for a period of years, the sensitive student would surely gain considerable empathy with perspectives other than his own. When he returns to his home country he will certainly be more understanding of the problems, methods, and goals of other countries and will be, in a significant sense, international. He will probably still identify most strongly with his own country, but he will see that country in an international context which he himself has experienced. The depth and scope of that perspective could not be matched by any national educational program because no national university could provide the intensity and diversity of the internationalizing experiences. To the extent that this perspective is a part of the international loyalty discussed earlier as a goal, that goal, too, is approached by a world university.

A world university could be popularly recognized as a symbol of coordinated, unified, human will to overcome the problems of mankind, a symbol of the internationality of knowledge and the drive to satisfy man's curiosity. Neutral nations could send their top students to such a university without identifying with one bloc or another, either in culture or in ideology.

In short, every goal ascribed to international higher education is within range of a world university, and its performance would be different in kind from that of any alternate program or national university. That difference in performance, resting as it does on the explicit internationality of the university, is the factor which justifies an interest in international higher education. Because there is an unmatched applicability of international higher education to the aims ascribed to it, the proposals we are about to study are as important as the goals to which they are addressed.

3 HISTORY

OF THE IDEA OF WORLD EDUCATION

I N 1919, the newly organized Union of International Associations, under the leadership of the Belgian educator Paul Otlet, founded the International University at Brussels.[1] The UIA immediately sought aid from the League of Nations, and it was because of the pressure of the UIA that the League first took steps to support international higher education. In July, 1920, the League Council directed the Secretary-General to urge member nations to aid the University in Brussels. Specifically, governments were asked to establish national chairs at Brussels where representatives could teach the culture and politics of their own nations. In a letter dated May 25, 1921, the Secretary-General of the League of Nations stated that "the co-operation of all states' members of the League of Nations in the work of the International Uni-

31

versity will greatly assist in forming an international public opinion capable of insuring the consolidation of the great institution which is entrusted to prevent the recurrence of . . . world war." [2] This letter constituted the most substantive support ever lent to international higher education by the League. Private correspondence between Otlet, his assistant Henri LaFontaine, and League officials indicates progressively increasing friction over financial support, with Otlet requesting it and the League continually explaining that moral suasion and suggestions were the extent of its powers. By 1927, the UIA seems to have given up all hope of financial support from the League of Nations.

But while the League did not act to give substantive aid to the International University at Brussels, it did hear debate among its own delegates as to the possible establishment of some other international college with League support. This discussion was centered in the Committee on Intellectual Co-operation (CIC), which first formally approached the question in 1922. The debate there was to continue until 1925 when, as we shall presently see, all plans for such universities were abandoned.

The cautious attitude and restrained approval exhibited by the League is typified in the remarks of Professor G. deReynold in the first session of the CIC. Beginning a proposal for an international conference of university personnel, he submitted that "the League of Nations, being the central organization for the coordination and control of international relations, is entitled to be informed of relations between universities, although it may not interfere with university teaching or infringe the sovereign right of states. . . . The League of Nations is authorized to make practical suggestions to universities and governments." [3]

CIC member J. Destree from Belgium wanted the Committee to express a desire for an international university, although he freely conceded such a "Utopian" program to be unfeasible at the time. "Professor deReynold was not blind to the importance of the question, but thought that it necessitated a profound preliminary study. M. Destree asked only that, for the benefit of posterity, note should be taken of the fact that, in 1922, someone had had the idea of an international university." [4] The question was set aside for another year, no provisions for "a profound preliminary study" having been made.

In late July, 1923, Professor D. N. Bannerjea, member of CIC, and professor of political economics at the University of Calcutta, brought to the Committee's attention "A Proposal for the Establishment of an International University under the Auspices of the League of Nations." [5] The title itself is of interest, as it answers deReynold's restrictive observation that the League could not "interfere with university teaching or infringe the sovereign rights of states." If the League could not dictate to national universities, then let the League operate its own university. This was necessary, according to Bannerjea, because "the reality of the League's achievements for the future must eventually be conditioned by the reality and sincere character of its efforts to embody progressive reforms in an international system of education which may be at once truly national and genuinely international without being cosmopolitan or unduly propagandistic. But such experiments can be fruitfully conducted by the League only in an institution directly under its control." [6]

Nowhere was the paradox of "truly national and genuinely international" explained, and it seems clear from these introductory remarks that national interests, expressed in the desire for the perpetuation of nationalism, still determined the proposals and activities of the League, even if those activities were to take place within its own university. This idea is further borne out in Bannerjea's assertion that success depended upon "efforts sedulously to steer clear of national interests and commitments" in the treatment of classroom material. Rather, the International University should focus its attention on the common points bridging

33

cultures. It should be "a nursery of international ideals, i.e., ideals of concord and harmony. . . ." Apparently, points of conflict were to be avoided. The words are almost tragic examples of the restrictions placed on education by nationalism. But Bannerjea, still hoping for a university, sought practical steps to bring about the "progressive reforms" needed. He suggested that the curriculum include "scientific study of oriental cultures," colonial and diplomatic history, and a section on comparative institutions. He also included "literature dealing with ways and means to promote cooperation between East and West on terms of honor, self-respect, and equality."

The University was to be located in some European academic center "conspicuous for its traditions of learning," and, initially at least, was to be structurally connected with the local and national university. " 'Ordinary' courses might be held at the latter university, the International University being free to concentrate its energies and efforts on its own peculiar work." It is not clear if Bannerjea thought of the university simply as a semi-independent department of international studies of the parent university, since his proposal does not describe the students or faculty of the international university, nor methods of their selection. The rather vague description of location is significant because it was made after recognizing the importance of setting the university in a place which could easily attract students. In this regard, Bannerjea's proposal anticipated one of the main obstacles to a successful international university, viz., immediate and solid recognition by the academic community. In more recent years, suggested solutions have pivoted more frequently on financial resources than on location, but Bannerjea's comments on location represent his most sophisticated insight.

The rest of his proposal, touching on the problems of finance and structure, is hardly helpful to one anxious for practical solutions. Funds for the university would be forthcoming almost automatically because the project was a good one. "Funds collected for the university may be administered by a trust composed of distinguished representatives of the countries concerned . . ." and "the appointing of a Governing Board and The Academic Council of the University is a matter clearly capable of adjustment." [7] Apparently, he saw little problem in obtaining an international charter as a legal structure, the charter to be issued by the League "with the consent of all its members." Seen in the light of future practical obstacles to a world university, Bannerjea's brief, hopeful sketches of structure and financial resources are weak and not at all characterized by the sophistication of his remarks on location. Neither the composition nor the method of appointment of the Governing Board or the Academic Council was touched upon, even though these matters are crucial to the satisfactory operation of the international university. But for all its insufficiency, Bannerjea's plan is the first official one to include practical suggestions to be brought before the League of Nations.

There followed, in September, 1923, another, briefer proposal from the Spanish government.[8] The suggestion for an "international autonomous university" was part of a three-point program submitted to the CIC. The other two sections concerned international recognition of secondary school diplomas and the establishment in each member state of "a higher educational center for all branches of higher study," whose diplomas were to be internationally valid. The diploma of the international university was also to be recognized in all states which were members of the League.

According to the Spanish proposal, the university was to be "established in one of the four universities of Christendom—Paris, Salamanca, Oxford, or Bologna . . . its professors would be selected from among the most distinguished intellectual and scientific personalities, regardless of their nationality." Like Bannerjea's, this plan would join the international university to a well-respected existing university, again probably to secure a maximum of academic pres-

35

tige and resources. But no further mention of details was included, the document being confined to "the general principles of the proposals, which . . . should be referred to the Committee on Intellectual Co-operation [for study] in conjunction with the proposals submitted by Professor Bannerjea. . . ." There is even less in this proposition than in Bannerjea's to make it concrete and to distinguish the university from a department of international relations of a national university. The CIC did eventually execute a study of international higher education, but not before the two plans already mentioned were supplemented by several others, presented at the third session of the Committee in December, 1923.

By far the most completely detailed of later proposals was that of the Greek National Committee,[9] submitted by Georges J. Remoundos, then professor at the National University and the National Polytechnical School of Athens. As pointed out in Chapter 1, the Greeks felt that the university "would greatly help towards the organization of mutual intellectual assistance," and to this end they suggested that "there should be only advanced research courses extending over one-half year, dealing with subjects not included in degree examinations of national universities." In addition to the program of research, the university would also convene "conferences of specialists," presumably to augment the research processes.

The university would also offer degree courses by correspondence, examinations being held simultaneously in the countries of all members of the League. As in the other proposals, the Greeks insisted that all degrees conferred be recognized by all League members. The courses given at national university campuses "should be organized and inspected by the National Committee of the country in which the university is situated."

The students of the university would be from the best of each participating country, and the faculty would be appointed by the League for a renewable term of six months. The major innovation of the Greek proposal was the suggestion that the faculty be of two types—those appointed for six months, and "permanent professors . . . who have retired from university work in their own country." No reason is given in the text, but the effort is to establish continuity with the permanent core while also providing a certain degree of freshness with the rapid turnover of the others. Most likely, however, the main reason for including the permanent staff was the desire to utilize an otherwise unused resource of experience, the population of retired professors.

The Rumanian National Committee also mentioned an international university, but failed to offer any definite suggestion after observing that "the realization of this idea seems extremely difficult, if not impossible." [10] With similar words, the Austrian National Committee declared that "in view of the political situation, the plan for establishing an International University was premature." [11] Instead, Austria recommended that an International University Information Office be created where national committees of the League might supply information about their national universities. Such an office was established by 1924.

In a similar vein, the Czechoslovak National Committee [12] wanted a central office to act as an "intermediary for the borrowing of books," to which university libraries would perhaps supply duplicate catalogues so that books could be located from all over the world. The Lithuanian National Committee, concerned for increased intellectual cooperation, [13] wanted an exchange system for objects of scientific interest, "especially zoological, botanical, and geological specimens."

At the end of the third session of the CIC, the Committee officially initiated the first study and report on the feasibility of international higher education. The study was undertaken to draw up a report for the Fifth Assembly of the League. It was decided that Bannerjea's, Otlet's, and the

Spanish proposals were all to be considered together, and Mr. O. deHalecki was designated to submit the report.

DeHalecki, professor at the University of Warsaw, tendered his findings in early 1924.[14] His fairly extensive discussion opposed the creation of a world university, and his statement remains one of the most articulate expressions of that opposition. Discussing some of the difficulties, deHalecki considered two cases: an independent, newly created university, as was Otlet's, and a new university as an appendage to some existing university, such as that proposed by Bannerjea. In the first case, only sizable financial support could create library and research facilities comparable to excellent standards, and deHalecki questioned the availability of such funds. He likewise questioned the supposition that national governments would accept such a university and divert funds from their own national educational systems.

On the other hand, he doubted that any national university would want an international appendage. Even if it were accepted, rivalries and jealousies between the international university and its host institution would be substantial. Either alternative would present a difficult and politically painful choice of location. Elaborating on the expected rivalry, he suggested that an "incontestably dangerous" situation would develop for national universities if the international university were to confer degrees "valid in all countries and substitutes for those given by the national universities." This point was part of an attack on internationalism and utopianism in general. More acceptable to deHalecki was "an institution offering post-graduate instruction dealing with subjects which are not generally included in national university programs." DeHalecki also claimed that "it would be disastrous" to separate research institutes entirely from traditional universities, and feared that a world university might effect at least a partial separation.

After considering the dangers of internationalism and the various practical blocks to the establishment of a world university, deHalecki concluded his attack, "It would seem from the technical difficulties and above all from the basic objectives raised by an international university that its essential advantages, as envisaged by its promoters, could more easily and more rapidly be obtained by a completely different method." The alternative suggested was the development and utilization of "presently existing elements of interuniversity co-operation, elements already proven by actual experience."

Having thus discussed international higher education as a means to desirable ends, and further, having criticized a fundamental goal of a world university itself, deHalecki went on to support his own alternative solution. To do so, he willingly borrowed those aspects of a world university which pleased him and set them in a different organizational structure. He approved of expanded exchange programs, but saw the difficulty of obtaining a thoroughly heterogeneous group. He hoped to solve the problem through a series of international summer seminars which were to bring students together from all over the world.

DeHalecki was sympathetic to the desire for increased study of international relations, and he admitted the value of conducting the study in an international body. But he proposed that the setting be provided at various national universities, each one specializing in some particular culture, research problem, or discipline. Each of the centers would be open to students and staff from many countries. Each center would be "created and maintained by the universities of the entire world . . . in a location most appropriate for each specialty." Special emphasis would be on research and postgraduate study not usually done at national universities, a curricular suggestion quite in keeping with a hesitation to compete with existing nationalism. As a result of the plan, deHalecki concluded, "one would arrive successively at the founding of increasingly numerous international university institutes common to all nations . . . the increasingly complete network of these institutes would constitute the relatively easiest realization of the international university, and the most useful at the same time." [15]

DeHalecki's report epitomizes the pattern of criticism most often expressed concerning the creation of a world university. Heavy emphasis is laid on the practical difficulties, approval is extended to at least some of the goals, and finally some alternative program is suggested. The program is also typical in that the alternatives put forth amount to an increased international exchange program among strengthened departments of national universities. The shortcomings and inappropriateness of these methods have already been treated in Chapter 2. We shall have occasion in Chapter 6 to discuss some of the practical difficulties of a world university and indicate possible solutions.

The express fear of internationalism was not unusual in debate on international education, and the feeling that a world university might create some supranational culture or power completely outside any national sphere repulsed many people in early talks. Besides deHalecki's castigation, the apprehension was made clear by an original sponsor of the Brussels International University in 1920. Mr. da Costa, Portuguese delegate to the Union of International Associations, expressed grave reservation before supporting Otlet's planned university. In da Costa's words, it was "necessary not to intercede in the development of each country according to its abilities and national qualities. We must not want to create a purely international organ which will produce absolutely nothing. It is necessary that each country be left with its own characteristics, and to use these qualities well to co-operate toward certain common goals." [16]

It does not seem from the proposals themselves, their context, or their stated purpose that the fear of internationalism in that sense was justified. Of the three proposals considered by deHalecki, certainly Otlet's was the most comprehensive in purpose and design, and the only one which might have been partially directed toward some supranationalism. Otlet himself meticulously, if somewhat glibly, denied this in remarks following da Costa's already quoted reservation, and at least the explicit purpose was aimed at affording increased international collaboration and a common international background. The fear of internationalism was surely completely unfounded in the Spanish proposal, which was motivated almost entirely out of a desire to see university degrees universally recognized. To the Spaniards, an international university, supported by all nations, would surely confer such a degree. The Greeks had already anticipated the conflict and suggested that the university only offer courses not a part of the ordinary national curriculum, a plan which deHalecki specifically approved as a resolution of the issue.

As we have seen in Bannerjea's presentation, he sought "sedulously to steer clear of national interests" in every way at the international university and envisioned educational reform "without being cosmopolitan." It is difficult to say whether these statements were made to ward off others' criticism, or if Bannerjea shared the fear of internationalism. In either case, the presence of the issue is clear in a large percentage of early debates, and is, perhaps, the most common feature beyond the concept of international education itself.

As part of his introductory comments,[17] deHalecki refers to correspondence received from the International Confederation of Students. It was the consensus of the ICS that the work of the world university as outlined in the Spanish proposal "would be totally identical with that of the regular universities. The Brussels International University promises a course of study completely different, complementary to regular universities, and one which seems more interesting to us." This is the only official statement of student expression on this whole question, with the recent exception of a United States National Student Association resolution in

41

1962 offering support to the Association for Commitment to World Responsibility in its project for a United Nations University. But the USNSA resolution was in no way incisive or critical in its expression, and merely offered its aid in literature distribution for ACWR.

DeHalecki's report was followed within a month by another statement expanding the Spanish government's proposal.[18] This statement was drafted by Mr. J. Castillejo, then Secretary-General of Spain's Junta Para Ampliacon de Estudios. After reading deHalecki's attack on international higher education, including the original Spanish proposal, Castillejo talked with the President of Spain and the undersecretaries of foreign affairs and public instruction for clarification of Spain's position. He was told that "the proposals . . . were of a general nature and hadn't been studied in detail. The government doesn't believe that these projects are immediately realizable." In this document, Castillejo affirmed that "learning should recognize no frontiers" and that the Spanish proposal "is a manifestation of a spirit which has prevailed in academic circles in Spain during the last twenty years." After this background, some "obstacles" to effective operation of a world university were noted, much along deHalecki's line of thought.

The first of the four impediments was the possible hesitation different nations might feel at sharing economically valuable information, such as new industrial processes or efficient methods of analysis. Of course, all military information would be stopped, and the university would be less effective as a central locus of meeting and exchange. Closely tied to this was the possibility, if not the certainty, of national jealousies and rivalries, whereby each participating nation would want to dominate and take credit for important work. These rivalries would be best countered by placing the university "under the control of the League of Nations," but the problem of neutrality was never resolved completely for Castillejo.

Further echoing the admonitions of deHalecki, this report continued to suggest that an international university, research center, or other academic institution would likely be offensive to existing national universities, largely because of its role as a competitor. One of the important manifestations of this rivalry might be the difficulty of getting national universities to give up their best professors to teach at the new international university. This variation on Bannerjea's fear that the new university would not attract top personnel became a popular objection to the world university in later years and does indeed constitute an important consideration, to be dealt with below.

After World War II, when national universities became to a greater degree international because of exchange programs and international studies centers, the suggestion for an international university to act in a capacity beyond the scope of national education was sometimes seen as an insult to national education programs. Before World War II, emphasis was placed on the development of research facilities and the like which would complement the work of national universities. However, after 1946, even the motive of complementation was viewed as rivalry to national universities, which now more and more felt themselves to be complete and sufficiently international.

The final obstacle mentioned in Castillejo's presentation is related to the problem of national jealousies. It was suggested that some nations might refuse to recognize the degree granted by the international university, again injecting the entire question of degree equivalence into the discussion. However, the possibility of refusal of degree recognition does not seem to be a fundamental obstacle, inasmuch as any nation participating or sponsoring the international university would certainly recognize its degrees. The same holds true for sponsoring academic associations or unions of universities. The real problem, of which degree refusal is only a symptom, is the lack of adequate academic and governmental support for the entire university, a lack which would stem directly from the feeling that the international university represented a danger to the national establishment, or that it usurped the proper domain of national universities. In later years, emphasis shifted heavily in this latter direction, even though the point was only hinted at in earlier opposition. The inclusion by Castillejo of the equivalence-of-degrees problem may indicate a desire on the part of one nation to achieve international recognition of its higher education degrees, using a world university as a means to that end.

To all of these obstacles, the only solution offered was the placing of the international university "under the control of the League of Nations." Beyond that, no discussion of the problem was conducted. But the new document did elaborate somewhat on the original Spanish proposal, extending it to include more than a world university. The first addition was the call for "gradual internationalization of the present universities," to be achieved through a three-point program: increasing exchanges of professors, not necessarily on a strictly reciprocal basis, among national universities; broad exchange of publications and bibliographies; and, not surprisingly, international recognition of secondary school diplomas by all universities. This latter provision is little more than an expedient for broader student exchange programs. Apparently, Castillejo also felt that existing universities could not be entirely satisfactory, so he envisioned "the foundation or development of international institutes of scientific research," a phrase never more fully explained. It would very likely have been a series of single-discipline research centers, each comparable to CERN.

Implying basic dissatisfaction with the bolstered, internationalized university, and after accounting for separate scientific research, the proposal continued to provide for a world school for the study of international social science problems. The school "should be founded at the seat of the League of Nations, at the center where all the elements of study will be concentrated, and where the problems to be settled will arise. . . . From this school would come the workers who in each country would guide the evolution toward a reign of peace and international co-operation." It is interesting that such a comprehensive proposal of structure was submitted, even though there was absolutely no indication of detail or method in the brief report. It allows for all levels of education for international understanding and cooperation, including exchange programs, publications, national universities, international research centers and an international university, basically oriented toward the social sciences. While this scheme does not resolve the fear of rivalry and jealousy, it does at least explicitly allow national programs and other similar means to work in cooperation with the world university. The proposal suggests alternative paths to the goal of cooperation and understanding, but its major drawback is the total absence of clear solutions to the problems posed.

Castillejo's report was brought to the attention of the CIC along with the deHalecki exposition. Meeting in its fourth session, July 25–29, 1924, the Committee reviewed these reports, the principles contained in them, and the practical objections raised. As a result of these studies, the Committee concluded that "obstacles, at the moment insurmountable, stand in the way of the immediate creation of an official international university." [19]

This rejection, however, did not leave the Committee without a policy regarding international education, or at least education for international understanding. The CIC went on to make alternate proposals, a move which it "deems to be its duty." The subsequent resolutions, all requesting voluntary action by national universities, were that

1] States and universities, while fully preserving their autonomy, to grant as far as possible the same value . . . to courses given by foreign professors on the invitation of the universities as to courses given by national professors;

2] Those states, universities, and scientific associations which possess institutes, to open them as far as possible to foreign students.

45

Beyond these, the Committee encouraged universities to open international study programs and departments, hoping that those departments would keep in touch with each other, possibly to effect exchanges among them.

To help administer the exchange program, a Subcommittee upon the Exchange of Professors and Advanced Students between Different Countries was created as an appendage to the Committee on Inter-University Co-operation, itself part of the CIC. The new subcommittee was "to inform itself fully regarding the score or more of agencies" which engaged in exchange programs and planning, to report the conditions and progress of these agencies, and to "devise new plans if it so desires." [20]

In its deliberations on the Castillejo and deHalecki reports, the CIC made no real attempt to study the obstacles with the hope of finding some solution consistent with an international university. No attempt was made, even by the original proposers, to formulate a possible structure for a world university which would do away with the many conflicts. In the attack on the idea no detailed correlation was even suggested between necessary characteristics of an international university and the obstacles and frictions it was supposed to raise. In short, opposition rested on a general charge of impracticality born out of a real lack of practical propositions on the part of the proponents of the idea.

Perhaps sensing the need for detail, Swedish Doctor R. Barany brought another plan before the CIC in 1925,[21] the Committee's previous rejection notwithstanding. In his "Scheme for the Establishment of an International University for the Training of Statesmen, Diplomats, Politicians, Political Editors and Professors in High Schools of Political Science," Barany noted that "a statesman should be acquainted not only with the interests of his own nation, but also—and to an equal degree—with the interests of the other nations. . . ." This would imply a course of studies including political history, comparative political economy, comparative constitutions and political administration, international law and the jurisprudence of the various nations, political psychology, and modern languages. This is the first mention of any detailed, explicit, coordinated curriculum which might be adopted by the international university, far surpassing the slight mention given the question by Bannerjea. The projected result of this curriculum would be "raising the level of political conscience of all nations."

The structure and administrative organization set forth also constituted the first substantive outline on the question ever put before the League of Nations. After declaring that the university should be "entirely autonomous, both politically and financially," a reasonably complete structure was suggested, including methods of selection in some instances. Barany's international university "would be governed by a Managing Board composed of leading men and women drawn from every part of the world and distinguished for their independence of thought and energy; this Board might co-opt other members. The rector, the secretary-general, and the deans of the university would also be members of the Board. The Board would elect the chancellor of the university, who would be its president. The chancellor would devote all his time to the university, whereas the members of the Managing Board would only meet at the university once a year for about a fortnight . . . [to] assure themselves that the teaching was being given in the spirit intended." While this detail represents important progress over previous plans, it still skirts the central problem, the selection process of the Managing Board. There is no indication as to Barany's thoughts on the question, and without the answer the added detail of this part of the proposal is without real basis. It is not enough to say that the good faith and international balance of the university president will be guaranteed by the internationality of his selection board unless that board is also of the good faith and balance desired. Some selection process must therefore be discussed.

Barany's treatment of the faculty is unmatched in any other proposal. He would divide the professors into two categories "Those teaching subjects unconnected with the nationality of the professor; those teaching the political history, history of civilization, political economy, or constitution and government of some particular nation. These [latter] chairs would be held by neutrals or by representatives of the nation in question who were free from all ultra-nationalistic tendencies." Provision for faculty selection was made, charging the chancellor with the duty of appointing or inviting faculty on the recommendations of either the Managing Board or "by the staff of professors where a sufficient number of chairs had been endowed." Once again, the crucial importance of a balanced Managing Board is apparent. For if the Board is partial in its appointments to any culture or ideology, the needed and invaluable balance in the faculty will be lost, crippling the university in the full pursuance of its goals.

Study directors, department heads, and other similar academic administrative personnel would be appointed by the faculty itself, naming professors from the existing staff or recruiting new people from other institutions. All recruitment would be subject to final approval of the university chancellor. All professors and study directors would serve an initial term of one year, during which "they would be on leave from their home institution. At the end of the one year they might be reappointed for a longer period."

According to the plan, instruction would be conducted "partly by lectures, and partly by the seminar system," the student spending five to six years in pursuit of a doctorate in political science, the degree conferred by the university. Transfer students would be allowed to enter from other graduate programs, with a system of credit transfer for similar courses. At the same time, it would not be necessary that all attending students continue until they earn the degree. In these regards, the international university would be,

48

in form, much like a national graduate program except that the staff, faculty, administration, and curriculum would be thoroughly international.

The international university was to be located in "a small neutral country." Specifically favored were Switzerland (Geneva), so near to the League of Nations and its resources, problems, and example; the Netherlands (The Hague), perhaps as an extension of the Academy of International Law. Besides these two centrally located countries, Norway and Sweden were mentioned because of the "existing interest in Peace" there. A secondary advantage to Scandinavia would be its relative remoteness from central Europe, thereby insuring its continued safety and operation in the event of another war.

The language was to be French, "the language of diplomacy," or English, although "lessons in all languages should be obtainable by students at a moderate charge." The proposed major languages offer no real surprise, but the notion of lessons in any language seems a little remote from possibility.

By an undefined process, Barany arrived at a proposed operating budget of $300,000,000 to cover expenses for an unspecified length of time. It certainly included more than the initial capital expenditures for buildings and equipment. The significant point in the discussion of finances was not the budget total but the suggested sources of funds, a consideration far more crucial than a precise monetary calculation. In all, Barany lists five possible money sources, each one simply mentioned with no further indication of relative merit. According to the proposal, money would be forthcoming from personal donations by wealthy "lovers of peace," as well as funds donated by peace organizations and governments. In addition to these sources, the general population might be stirred through newspaper fund-campaigns carried on around the world; the remainder of the funds to be collected by the sale of a pamphlet describing "the importance

49

of the creation of an international university." While the $300,000,000 figure is unexplained, there is no doubt that this cataloguing of financial sources is more conducive to affirmative reaction than Bannerjea's naive dismissal of the problem on the grounds that the idea would somehow automatically attract funds.

Very little is said about students in this report. No mention is made of selection, although some attention is given to defining the question of student housing, a matter heretofore neglected. Barany had two proposals for student accommodation, students quartered either along national lines, or in a thoroughly mixed, international fashion. No preference is indicated, nor are the relative merits at all explored. Otherwise, the university was to be coeducational, maintain "a large library," and offer "large numbers" of scholarships. Barany also envisioned a student newspaper, and even went so far as to insist explicitly that "dwelling should be strictly forbidden."

The Barany proposal emerged as the most complete and most sophisticated ever brought to the League of Nations for direct implementation. Its advantage was that it indicated *possible* solutions to problems, while making no claim to offer unique solutions. At least there was something substantive to discuss regarding method. These indications might easily be taken as promising signs of ultimate practicality and thereby spur on further study.

The CIC did formally discuss this proposal,[22] the debate finally resulting in two resolutions designed again to undermine the proposal and the idea of international higher education. The major participants in the discussion were Destree and deReynold, the former supporting the concept in general, the latter opposed to the whole program and its motivation. Destree recognized the need for an international university to educate in the area of politics, but felt that any other disciplines included in the curriculum would be unnecessary and undesirable duplication of work done at national universities. He therefore asked that some kind of international university be established with a structure similar to existing higher schools of political science. A student body of one hundred would study for three years, spending a year in each of three cities: Paris, London, and Berlin. This idea of rotating location was a new one, which somehow never was expressed in later formulations.

Following Destree's remarks, deReynold repeated the old warning that it was "essential to avoid schemes which might encourage utopianism and internationalism." Not wishing to be entirely negative, he noted that steps should be taken to assure the increased translation and dissemination of more accurate information. DeReynold's position was summed up in a resolution adopted by the Committee, encouraging study of the development of international collaboration: "*a*] by the education of journalists and translators; *b*] by prolonged courses for students in the principal foreign universities; *c*] by instruction in the various national histories; *d*] by the measures defined in the resolution of the Inter-University Sub-Committee in April, 1924."

The resolution referred to [23] named six measures to be undertaken in the pursuit of international cooperation and understanding. They included exchange of professors and students, international equivalence of diplomas, courses on contemporary nations and politics, the teaching of modern languages, and some type of international study during vacations. All these programs were to be conducted by national universities, the League of Nations simply offering the suggestion and expressing the desire for implementation by others.

The passivity of the League exemplified in these resolutions was the real reason that it took no action to support international higher education. The organization did not feel strong enough or independent enough from nationalism to back actively a major innovation in education. Rather, it felt

51

bound to give advice and exert moral suasion in the hope
that existing institutions would somehow adapt themselves
to meet the needs of complex international relations. For the
League actively to support the idea of a world university,
with no possible means of mustering support for its independent implementation, would be fruitless and an embar-
rassing indication of the League's real impotence.

This view is reflected in Destree's resolution concerning
Barany's plan. Now faced with a detailed outline of proposed structure, curriculum, faculty, and finances, the
CIC could no longer dismiss international higher education as patently unfeasible, as it had done the year before.
Nor did it choose to reopen its study of feasibility to include
and expand Barany's suggestions. Instead, the Committee
adopted a resolution which observed that Barany's plan
"goes beyond the limits of the schemes to be considered at
the present moment," implying that the League could not
take positive steps once a feasible plan was brought to its
attention. The resolution was supported by Destree, who
observed that Barany's idea was "too big." This is, of course,
a complete reversal of previous rejections of plans as too
weak and incomplete.

In order to keep the concept of international higher education from withering completely, Destree's resolution noted
that the basic idea was a good one and "asks the International Institute at Paris to investigate these questions." The
Committee on Intellectual Co-operation adopted this resolution, thereby divorcing itself finally and completely from all
further responsibility for the creation of a world university.
The International Institute never considered the question,
and Destree's resolution marks the last known consideration
of international higher education by the League of Nations
or any other nonprivate organization until the end of World
War II.

4 PROPOSALS

TO INTERNATIONAL BODIES

AFTER THE League of Nations abandoned the idea of international higher education, no other international organization actively considered a world university until late in 1945, when preparatory committees met in London to plan the development of the United Nations Educational, Scientific and Cultural Organization (UNESCO). Records of the first plenary sessions [1] allude to several suggestions concerning international higher education, notably one submitted by Jaime Jaramillo-Arango on behalf of the Colombian government. The proposal came in a letter to Sir Alfred Zimmern, Secretary-General of the conference, and observed that "the University should have a certain number of permanent chairs and that others might be equipped with Lecturers and Visiting Professors belonging to the United Nations

53

who would render assistance to the University in their turn . . . the same idea of rotation should govern the fixing of scholarships, of which it is hoped there will be many."

The envisioned faculty structure is not unlike that suggested by Greece in 1923, although here the rotating faculty seemingly would be staffed by practical men, taken directly from field work with the United Nations, as opposed to more academically oriented people considered in the earlier proposal. There is much continuity of thought between presentations to the League and to UNESCO, with occasional reference and frequent duplication of ideas. But from the very beginning of UNESCO consideration of international universities, even in the Colombian letter, there is an emphasis on practicality unmatched in earlier years. Most important, practicality was being urged by proponents of international education in answer to the devastating review of the idea written by deHalecki for the Committee on Intellectual Co-operation. After 1945, supporters of world education took the offensive. A most important element of this new approach was the insistence that the United Nations or UNESCO become directly involved in the support, if not control, of any world university established.

This new direction is evidenced even in the title of the Colombian proposal, "A University of the United Nations," implying a degree of relationship between the University and the UN far more intimate than the degree of interaction expected from the League. Not even Otlet wanted more than financial support from the League, aid which was never forthcoming. But after the war, UNESCO, the newly created international agency which was to aid and develop national education, was also being sought to do for internationalism that which the League of Nations never did. Further, UNESCO was sought as a prime mover in international education rather than a supporter of privately generated projects.

If post-World War II proposals were generally more vitally concerned with involving the resources and prestige of international organizations, and if the proposals of the forties showed more awareness of practical obstacles than those brought to the CIC, these later plans were no more concrete in actual outline of action than the vague suggestions doomed in the twenties. Jaramillo-Arango, after hinting at a possible faculty structure, with no mention of ways to make it operational, closed his letter to Zimmern with the remark, "I cannot, of course, and do not wish in this note, to enter into technical details." The extent of this apparent disdain among proponents for "technical details" is difficult to assess, but, just as the League of Nations before it, UNESCO was not yet to hear detailed and well-constructed proposals for international universities. Once again, proposals were limited to general statements of need, with at best vague references to structure. The new recognition of practical problems by proponents of international education seems to have driven them to insist that UNESCO adopt the difficult project in the hope that UNESCO might somehow come up with the solution. In the closest continuation of League tradition, the Colombian project and others brought to UNESCO through early 1946 were "recommended for further study to the Preparatory Commission." [2]

There is one exception to these cursory proposals. Deposited with the Executive Committee of the Preparatory Commission in November, 1945, was "A Proposal to Establish a University of the United Nations," described by its authors as "a petition to the United Nations from members of the armed forces in Rome, Italy." It was prepared by an *ad hoc* group of Americans, Britons, and Italians, its private character differing from the official government statements which made up the bulk of the Commission's material. Even though private, it is mentioned here because it was carefully considered by the early UNESCO planners, receiving attention equal to that of other proposals, and was far more carefully treated than subsequent private proposals deposited at UNESCO.

As envisioned, the University of the United Nations

would be open to graduate students working for master's or doctorate degrees and would offer those degrees, although students could attend for shorter periods with no obligation to work toward a final degree. Great curricular emphasis would be placed on comparative international studies, almost exclusively in the social sciences and humanities, but including some work in law and languages. Very detailed subject matter is suggested within each of the categories, ranging from comparative mineral law to ethnology, mental hygiene, and twenty-eight languages. Instruction at the university would be in English, French, and Russian. By no means considered a definitive list by its authors, the one hundred and two suggested courses are prefaced with the observation that "the curriculum and the award of degrees will have to be planned carefully by whatever planning committee is appointed by UNESCO."

It is made quite clear that UNESCO should be the sponsor of the new university. This would involve the initial appointment of a "Board of Trustees to be composed of men well known in international education who will be assigned the task of studying carefully the proposal, in consultation with men who are expert in the organization and administration of graduate schools." These men would draw up a detailed plan of the university and, if approved by UNESCO, present that plan to the General Assembly of the United Nations for its approval.

The preparatory committee was reminded that "great care should be taken in preparing and presenting this proposal to the Assembly, for a poor presentation might 'kill' the idea at the first hearing. The persons delegated to make the presentation should be familiar with all of the details, be prepared to answer every criticism, and be able to explain the reasonableness of every proposal."

Once approved by the Assembly of the United Nations, those nations who wished to participate would supply funds and send students. Only those nations making contributions would retain the right to use the facilities of the university or send a national to study there. With sufficient support forthcoming, the Trustees and UNESCO would appoint a president, or rector, "who will then be charged with the responsibility of administering the university and the selection of the faculty and administrative staff." Operating costs would come from supporting nations and the UNESCO budget. Having thus outlined the structure, content, and financial resources of the university, the supporters turned their attention to the faculty. Chosen by the president with the help of the Trustees and national academic societies, faculty members should be academically excellent as well as personable, "international-minded," and dedicated to the United Nations. After a certain length of service, professors would achieve tenure, and pensions would be provided for the retired.

While all participants together would represent all areas of the world, the university itself would be located in some "small, centrally located" European country. First choice went to Switzerland because of the presence there of the United Nations, providing a model of internationalism and an ideal location for research on international problems. Men and women would be housed in dormitories, much like the campus housing of an American residential university.

The students attending the University's lectures, seminars, and tutorials would come from all countries and be, as much as possible, "potential public servants or opinion-influencing agents." The former include government officials at all levels; the latter teachers, journalists and others of the mass media, and clergymen. Having completed the course of study, these students would return home "to become active agents, strategically located, either to share their findings with the peoples of their nations, or to carry out their own professional work *with greater understanding, convictions and vision* of the many international problems now critically before the nations."

Submitted for the group by Professor A. B. Trowbridge,

then of the American Red Cross, this optimistic proposal was by far the most outstanding and detailed analysis of the problem UNESCO was to see for years. Each area of practical difficulty was briefly discussed, indicating possible but not definitive solutions. It was a model proposal, a straightforward, sincere, and unsolicited effort. Nothing was done with it.

Another early mention of world education came in February, 1946, when the Chinese delegation petitioned the UNESCO Preparatory Commission to include international higher education in the UNESCO program, then being formulated. China requested that "a number of United Nations Universities . . . be established . . . at least one on each continent." [3] In addition, China called for an expanded international exchange of students and faculty, a "United Nations Translation Bureau . . . to translate and make available the classics and other important works from different languages," and United Nations Libraries on every continent. The Translation Bureau, it was suggested, might work with the United Nations Universities to achieve "a standardization of scientific and other terms in different languages."

Just as the Colombian project, this one exhibits the same form and content as those proposals brought to the League, again with the important new emphasis on the active role to be played by UNESCO. The familiar pattern of the official proposal is seen here, beginning with a brief statement of need, continuing with a still more abbreviated review of possible structure and operation, and ending with hope and the recognition of the potential role of other programs, notably exchange programs of students and faculty. However, the Chinese suggestion that there be a series of regional universities anticipates the present feeling of many, that such a structure will be needed to avoid the problems of great cultural diversity which would necessarily be part and parcel of a single, world-encompassing educational institution. In Chapter 6 the implications, practical and theoretical, of this and alternate structures will be discussed in some detail.

Besides the Chinese and Colombian plans, the Appendix to the "Memorandum of the Education Program of UNESCO" [4] alludes to "a great many recommendations for the establishment of an international university in Geneva, New York, Washington, Rome, Salzburg and elsewhere." Reference is made to other plans similar to the Chinese series of universities, as well as to the establishment of a University of Europe. But the Memorandum itself [5] did not include international higher education in its prospective "Field Work and Staff Contacts," because "it is necessary to explore this matter over a period of time before wise action can be determined."

The results of one such exploration were published as part of the documents of the first session of the UNESCO General Conference, held in November, 1946. In a staff pamphlet entitled "Project for a UNESCO Educational Center," extensive attention was drawn to the need for developing international understanding, and among the suggested programs to "promote true international understanding" was a School of International Contacts. It was to be an annual summer program through which about one hundred graduate students from around the world might be brought together and into contact with an international faculty. Instruction would come from a series of lectures and discussions, subject material "drawn from the social and political life of the present-day world."

More like a high-level annual international symposium than a university, the School of International Contacts was explicitly "not to provide systematic instruction in any branch of study." The program was at all times to be bilingual, although the two languages were not made definite, nor was proposed location made less vague than that place where the school could "draw upon the services of a number

59

of persons who have had experiences of international affairs in different fields of activity."

The very small summer-session symposium envisioned is quite similar to the privately established international education experiments which came in the early 1960's and is identical in structure with Otlet's unsuccessful Brussels International University. While none of them is a university in any sense of the word, being far too limited in size and diversity, each was presented in the hope that something much bigger would develop. The operation of a pilot project to iron out difficulties deserves attention, and was most recently done in the United States in 1963, when, under the direction of Professor Harold Taylor, the Committee on a Friends World College brought together twenty-two students from as many countries and an international faculty of six on a campus near New York City. These pilot projects, all private, will be explored in detail in the next chapter.

The final "Report on the Program of UNESCO for 1946,"[6] delivered to the first General Conference of UNESCO for approval, included provision for "a further study of the problem of an international university" as one of the "Projects to be Undertaken in 1947."[7] The General Conference had slightly different ideas, however, and in December, 1946, its Sub-Commission on Education moved "that the project concerning an international university . . . be separated from the projected survey on training in international relations, and linked up with the study of Education for International Understanding."[8] The following day, "training in international relations, with particular reference to an International Study Center and an International University, was referred to the Social Sciences Sub-Commission."[9]

Partly because of this juggling of bureaucratic responsibilities, and partly because of the initial inefficiencies of operation in any new agency as large as UNESCO, an earlier study mandate from the Executive Committee of the

Preparatory Commission [10] was not acted upon for nearly two years. In October, 1946, the Executive Committee had requested that the Director General of UNESCO ask Sir Alfred Zimmern "to begin forthwith, in consultation with universities and specialized groups, a study of the possibilities of creating within the orbit of UNESCO a center for the study of international relations." It was exactly such a study of feasibility which was desired by all proponents of the world university, and the study was to seek ways of involving UNESCO in a most direct manner with the study center.

The meeting of university personnel, chaired by Zimmern, did not take place until August, 1948, in Utrecht. After several sessions, the conference finally agreed to endorse a series of international studies departments at national universities, each department to include scholars, professors, and educators of many nations, "provided that such departments should consist in part of scholars, professors and educators of the country in which the university is located." [11] This last qualification is a manifestation of continued fear of internationalism and the overbalancing of national perspective, a fear now expressed by educators instead of politicians.

The results of the Utrecht conference were not relevant to the original mandate for the meeting, since debate nowhere referred to the possibilities of creating an international center under the auspices of UNESCO. Resolutions passed by the conference included references to this lack of success in discussing the central question and mentioned an International Social Science Institute to be discussed in March, 1949. But no provisions were made for these discussions, nor was any further notice given in Utrecht to the question of such institutes. In fact, whatever meetings were contemplated for March, 1949, never took place. Instead, it was 1951 before UNESCO organized its next investigation into the possibilities of international higher education.

The year 1947 was not totally devoid of activity related to a world university, even though the 1946 UNESCO mandate to Zimmern was not immediately realized. The United Nations itself, through the Economic and Social Council, also considered the problem of international research centers as a special case of international higher education. An ECOSOC resolution in 1946 had called on the Secretary-General of the United Nations to collaborate with UNESCO on "the problem of the creation of United Nations Research Laboratories." The resolution pointed out "that a number of research projects do not seem to be able to be conducted in a rational fashion except at the international level." [12]

Henri Laugier, then Assistant Secretary-General of the United Nations, took responsibility for carrying out the mandate. Early in 1947, he sent a copy of the ECOSOC resolution to educators, research workers, academicians, political and social leaders, and academic associations around the world, asking each to comment on the proposed laboratories. The responses filled 441 pages of the official *Rapport du Secretaire General sur le Problème de la Création des Laboratoires de Recherches des Nations Unis*, filed in January, 1948.[13] The summary reports that "many of the institutions and persons consulted have expressed ardent approbation." Each country wanted to see a number of problems studied at the international level, and specialists in each academic discipline expressed desire for international coordination on at least some problems in their field. Among the subjects often singled out for international study were meteorology, soil erosion and other agricultural matters, geology, cancer and brain research, and a host of political and economic questions.

In July, 1947, the Society for the Psychological Study of Social Issues, a division of the American Psychological Association, responded to Laugier's letter with a draft proposal for a United Nations Institute of the Human Sciences. Although not a blueprint for the Institute, the report sets forth a series of objectives toward which the Institute might work, including the definition of research standards and equalization of research facilities, planning and coordination of research, and collection and dissemination of information. It also suggests a number of research topics, among them barriers to international communication and the best way to conduct international research. The Institute would be staffed mostly by year-term appointments of outstanding scholars, with care to avoid a continuous drain of personnel from any particular university or region.

Little resulted from this flurry of ECOSOC activity. In August, 1949, a committee of experts met to discuss the entire question of United Nations Research Laboratories. Rensis Likert, President of the Society for the Psychological Study of Social Issues when it responded to Laugier's letter, was a member of the committee, as was Laugier himself, representing the United Nations Secretary-General. The committee agreed again that it would be desirable and important to establish United Nations Research Centers, notably to delve the secrets of the brain and to study the complex problems of international political relations. Having thus expressed moral support for the institutes, the committee and ECOSOC left it to UNESCO to work out the details of the enabling procedure. Once again, the refusal to take up practical matters resulted in a resolution of principle never realized in deed.[14]

A UNESCO Seminar on Education for the Development of International Understanding also drafted a statement favorable to an international university, concluding that a world university would "encourage the growth of a new mental attitude, without which there can be no international understanding . . . the national university can never avoid a national outlook in the teaching of their disciplines." [15] UNESCO and the League of Nations had never before been so openly aware of, and distressed by, the limits of national education. In an ominous warning, it was noted that "in [pre-Nazi] Germany high cultural institutions such as research centers were no less developed than elsewhere. It is therefore not enough that peace-loving nations should develop and perfect their universities. They must do this in such a way that they are contributing to the development of . . . a spirit of peace."

According to the sketchy plan presented, "the best students from national universities would study there [at the world university]," although nothing was said about their selection nor was there mention of the faculty. Continuing the concern which dominated League debates, the diplomas of the international university were to be recognized in all countries which participated in the university. Commenting on the difficult problem of language, the report proposed that students be allowed to write papers in their native language, although classes would be conducted in French or English, the official languages of the university. In the instruction, "crystallization of all dogmas should be avoided and the frequent renewal of teachers and methods permitted."

While the proposal does not explicitly describe a series of international universities throughout the world similar to the Chinese plan presented the year before, something similar was implied by the proposed structure of the entire university. The whole would be split into two functionally distinct branches, one for study and formal education, the other devoted to research. The former branch would include several "institutes" of comparative studies, including sociology, pedagogy, economics, political science, anthropology and other disciplines in the social sciences. The latter branch would consist of a number of "research centers" for scholars and technicians, where such diverse topics as cancer, the causes of war, uses of solar energy, and community planning would be examined for new approaches and methods. No indication is given of the number or location of these centers and institutes, nor is the degree of cooperation among them discussed. Another problem implicit in a series of research centers, a question not mentioned in the report but later to be the topic of some concern, is the scope of research conducted at any one center. Shall each be single-disciplined, or shall each be devoted to a specific problem or fairly well-defined concern, calling upon experts in whatever fields needed for analysis of the problem? A third possibility, combining the two others, would establish one or several cross-disciplinary centers which would study problems in a number of fields simultaneously.

These alternatives were presented in 1951 to a conference of experts called by the Director General of UNESCO at that time, Jaime Torres Bodet, still following the mandate of 1946 to study the feasibility of a UNESCO-sponsored "center for the study of international relations." Delivering the brief keynote address [16] at UNESCO headquarters in Paris, Bodet emphasized the structural choices open to planners of international social science institutes. Appraising each, he said that a single large multi-discipline, multi-topic institute "would facilitate a 'world synthesis,' a comparison of all methods, all data and all results." He was, however, cognizant of the problems in such a structure, one of which would be "to introduce order into its activities which might all too easily be confused."

Terming a series of single-discipline institutes "a more cautious and perhaps more wise solution," Bodet nonetheless pointed out that such a structure "would deprive us of one immense advantage—daily cooperation between the various sciences in the analysis of problems . . . [which] cannot properly be analyzed from one standpoint alone, or by methods characteristic of a single discipline." Between these two partially unsatisfactory structural possibilities, Bodet saw and favored a third, less unwieldy than one large institute yet cross-disciplinary enough to gain as much interaction and synthesis as possible. His preference went to a series of cross-disciplinary single-issue centers of research, where "representatives of several disciplines . . . would be entrusted with the study of a given problem—youth, for instance, or technology."

Following the keynote address, the conference met and debated for three days, chaired by sociologist Robert Angell of the United States. It was finally recommended [17] that at least one cross-disciplinary but single-issue oriented International Social Science Research Center be established by UNESCO, although UNESCO sponsorship was in no way to interfere with the free academic independence of thought and activity at the Center. The final report stressed the training of internationally minded research workers, as well as the execution of high-level research by experts from around the world. Apparently, the training of new people would be accomplished through their employment as research assistants rather than through course work. The training envisioned in this report assumes the thorough academic background of the research assistants.

The exact combination of disciplines needed at each center would be determined by the specific issue under study, and all centers would be coordinated centrally by a governing board. The method of selection of this governing board is the most important addition made by this conference, because it indicates for the first time the precise manner in which high-level personnel might be chosen so that they would be acceptable to the academic community and UNESCO (or the sponsoring agent) at the same time. Each international academic association in the social sciences would nominate two candidates from its own membership who would best represent the interests of the discipline. One from each association would then be chosen to serve on the governing board, although he would serve as an individual, not as a direct representative of the international organization which nominated him. The method of selection among the nominees was not made explicit, but it was implied that this should be done by UNESCO personnel, either the Director General or his assistant for educational affairs. Final approval might be left to the UNESCO Executive Board. Once appointed for some specified term, the governing board would invite members of the world academic community to participate in whatever research projects were being conducted at the time. The board would also have authority to initiate new projects, and would be responsible for the general operation of the research centers.

After setting down this method of selection for a governing board and charging the board with all further responsibilities, the committee under Angell listed five areas of immediate social concern which it felt needed study at the ISSRC. Listed in the priority assigned them, they were: 1] the human implications of technical change; 2] formation of mass opinion; 3] international migration; 4] antagonisms between centers of political power; 5] problems of literacy and fundamental education. Ideally, each was to be explored at a different institute, with the committee estimating general operating expenses for each institute to be $300,000 per year. To provide continuity and decrease the possibilities of political manipulation, the committee did insist that each center have a five-year budget. The source of financial support was not discussed.

UNESCO did not take positive action to create the International Social Science Research Center, the subject of the 1951 conference of experts, nor did the various international academic associations carry the project further by themselves. But if this conference marked the end of UNESCO's attempts to create international social science centers for study and research, similar conferences involving UNESCO soon were to result in the establishment of CERN (Centre Européen des Recherches Nucléaires) as a single-discipline research center in physics.

This exploring of research centers, while highly important insofar as it manifests increasing concern over the limitations of national institutions, still does not focus on the ultimate goal of international universities where research is carried on with course work and full-time students in residence. Even the broadest research institute discussed by Bodet would not have been a university. This is not to suggest that CERN or any other international research institute, single- or cross-disciplinary, is not making or cannot make important contributions to international cooperation and understanding. But if we are to have an international university and center of graduate studies, we must look beyond CERN, beyond any institute, no matter how broad, which is dedicated solely to research.

After the development of CERN in 1954, the focus of UNESCO educational projects shifted to primary and secondary education. Still seeking international understanding, it sponsored the Associated Schools Project in Education for International Understanding and Cooperation, discussed in Chapter 2. But private individuals and groups have continued to send requests and proposals to the UNESCO Department of Education asking it to initiate an international university, and informal conjecture concerning a world university still arises occasionally within the department. Those who have taken ideas to UNESCO have done so in the hope that that organization would best be able to initiate a program as large and costly as a world university. The resources and prestige of UNESCO have been sought as attractions to internationally known men, and as support for superior research facilities and academic prestige which must immediately be the hallmark of a new international academic experiment.

In the past forty years, two international organizations directly concerned with education and international understanding have been approached by people seeking support for international higher education. Superficially, the end results have been indistinguishable, both the League and

UNESCO having responded negatively. But the obstacles of the twenties, passivity and fear of internationalism, had both diminished by the fifties, leaving inertia, jealousy, and doubts of academic and political practicality as the central nature of more modern opposition. Certainly UNESCO's stated purpose "to *initiate* desirable and important projects, including international research projects, [and] to *operate* programs in fields not adequately provided for, or where an international agency such as UNESCO is best fitted to work," [18] is far from the familiar League passivity and indicates a potential willingness to cooperate with would-be initiators. It constitutes an invitation for new ideas.

A striking example of the newly emerging disillusionment with national values as a basis for world organization is found in another part of the preparatory committee's 1946 statement. "Of all the problems falling within the field of the social sciences, none is more critical for the peace and well-being of the world than the emergence of a living and creative internationalism. The values of nationalism, particularly in holding a people together and enabling it to attain a distinctive culture, are everywhere appreciated and cherished. But if these values are to survive in the world of the future, an effective and substantial international framework must be devised. What is needed is a constructive analysis of the methods and institutions by which the positive values of nationalism can be extended into the international sphere." [19]

Here is a promising departure from the conservatism of the League, and while the view expressed is neither widespread nor has it resulted in the establishment of an international center for the further development of similar views, it marks the beginning of a willingness to depart from traditional standards and extend the best of today's thinking into new and different institutions. This departure alone is probably the most significant difference between the League of Nations and UNESCO. It is this new willingness, this potential for new direction, which has recently spurred some to reopen communication with UNESCO, and caused others to hope that UNESCO might take up private projects once begun. At least it can be said that the establishment of a world university by UNESCO is neither beyond that organization's accepted scope of activity, nor is it inconsistent with UNESCO's stated principles. What remains is the issue of feasibility. We now turn to this problem and review the history of private thought and pilot projects in international higher education.

5

SOME PROJECTS AND EXPERIMENTS

WHILE DIPLOMATS and committees of experts considered the prospects of international higher education through informal letters, petitions and reports to the League of Nations and UNESCO, other less official groups conducted private campaigns and occasionally even launched pilot projects of international universities. Except for Rabindranath Tagore's international experiment, Visva Bharati, in Santiniketan, India during the 1920's, all organized nongovernmental activity in support of international higher education has emanated from Europe and the Western Hemisphere. Tagore invited intellectuals from many countries to lecture at his institute and for several years conducted a series of seminars on world issues with small groups of students, mostly from India. In the Western world, some pilot projects were established, lectures and seminars were conducted on a small scale. But none of these efforts has fully materialized into a self-assured, academically recognized international university. In addition to the experimental establishments, more than a dozen paper projects have been turned out since 1945, urging the public or UNESCO to rally behind a world university or a series of international research centers. In nearly every instance, the hope of the private individual or group has been to gain some measure of support from official bodies, like UNESCO, although not all have wanted UNESCO or the League to control the entire operation of the university.

In general, private efforts have exemplified two crucial aspects of the activity for international higher education. First, it is evident from the work done and from comments which that work has elicited, that important and respected private foundations, educators, scholars, and businessmen, as well as student organizations, would welcome an international university. In nearly every quarter where the idea has been expressed, it has been favorably, often enthusiastically, received. Although plans and hopes for a world university have not had wide circulation among academic, cultural, and political circles of the world, the degree of support which those plans have found even with limited circulation suggests that widespread and strong popular backing for the idea is possible. The fact that a number of proposals were written without knowledge of other work in the field is further indication that popular support would be forthcoming and that there already exist a number of spontaneous movements all tending in the same direction.

Besides indicating to politicians and diplomats that private foundations, academic personnel, and scholars are interested in international higher education and would support official actions in that direction, many privately composed plans offer details of structure, finance, and other practical aspects of a world university far beyond the statements included in official government or UNESCO pronouncements. It would be difficult to overstate the importance of such practical discussions, especially for so complex an undertaking as a new university. No amount of theorizing will convince political men that a project is worth undertaking unless a detailed account of feasible procedure is also presented. It is this kind of an account which has been missing from official statements and has caused many people to become skeptical as to practical possibilities for a world university.

The plans discussed in this chapter may not be the most effective solutions to many problems, but they are an indication that tentative conclusions, displaying a considerable degree of plausibility, can be reached. Their importance lies not so much in the degree of relevance of the suggested plan but in the role of the plan as a tangible point of departure for further, more fruitful discussion. The proposals described, therefore, reflect a great amount of public support for a world university as a small step forward in the peaceful solution of man's problems and the satisfaction of his curiosity. Beyond that, their occasionally detailed analysis of practical impediments is an important point of reference. In both respects, the private activity recounted here is of some significance.

Shortly after World War I, the Union of International Associations called a conference to discuss the needs for an international university. Meeting in Brussels, the assemblage, primarily educators, concluded that there was indeed an important role for such a university to play in the postwar world. The conference named Paul Otlet to head a committee to draft plans for an international university, to be created under the auspices of the UIA. Assisted by Henri LaFontaine, Otlet wrote and presented a draft constitution and curriculum to another conference of the UIA, called in 1920. No more succinct statement of purpose, structure, and financial support for the university is to be found than the final draft of the Statute of the University, quoted in full below.

STATUTE OF THE UNIVERSITY

In order to assist in giving the intellectual forces their due share in the organization of international life and to further by the foundation of an institution the movement for the interchange of University Teachers and Students from the different countries:

1] The Universities and institutions of higher education undersigned or subsequently adhering to the present statute,

2] The International Associations undersigned or subsequently adhering to the present statute,

3] The Union of International Associations which, in co-operation with these Associations, has organized an International Center and placed its services at the disposal of the League of Nations,

4] The International Associations and Federations of Students and the International Confederation of Students,

have hereby constituted the International University which shall be governed by this Statute and whose aim shall be to carry out the various objects set forth in the ensuing program.

1 Aim and Organization

The International University shall aim at uniting, in a movement of higher education and universal culture, the Universities and International Associations. It will enable a proportion of students to complete their education by initiating them into the international and comparative aspects of all great problems. With this end in view, it shall organize annually a number of courses and lectures, if possible at its seat or in such other place as may be selected by common agreement. The sessions shall be completed by a University Tour systematically organized by the different Universities.

74

At these sessions, Universities will be invited to send their professors and lecturers, to expound the general results of their researches in courses of lectures. The International Associations shall be invited to make known through their authorized representatives the present state of the most important questions in which they are engaged, the Nations to endow chairs for the study of their respective countries, institutions and civilization.

The University shall also act as a center for higher educational studies and scientific, technical and social research. Laboratories and Institutes may be associated with it. In particular, it will serve to establish the most complete agreement between the principles which control the evolution of civilization and the development of the League of Nations.

II *Members*

The members of the International University shall be:
1] Corporate bodies: Universities, Higher Educational Institutions and International Associations
2] Individuals: University Teachers and Students

III *Administrative Machinery*

Pending the organization of the International University, which shall not exceed two calendar years, it shall be administered by a committee of 21 members elected by the Universities, Higher Educational Institutions and Associations being collective members of the International University. Each member shall be entitled to one vote. The Committee shall elect from its number an executive committee of three. The committee shall be responsible for drawing up its own standing orders.

Two delegates shall be elected, as members of the said Committee, respectively by the Teaching Staff and the Students as soon as these bodies can meet.

The Union of International Associations shall place its administrative machinery at the disposal of the International University until the International University be fully organized.

The first revision of the Statute, under Article XIII, shall provide for the actual administrative machinery of the International University. The election of the provisional Committee shall be conducted by correspondence before March 1, 1921, at the instance of the committee of the Union of International Associations.

IV   Legal Status

The University is constituted as an international association, under the terms of the Belgian Act, October 25th, 1919, granting "Capacite Juridique" to international associations that have no pecuniary end. . . .

V   Students and Associates

The international university primarily appeals to students of both sexes intending to supplement the education received in Universities and Higher Educational Institutions. Further it appeals to all wishing to equip themselves efficiently for the higher offices in International Administration or in the League of Nations as well as for any other career in which an extensive training in international questions is necessary or desirable. Finally it offers adequate means of studying to all desiring to keep abreast of professional progress or to enlarge their general culture.

VI   Courses of Study

The courses of study shall comprise instruction in the doctrines and various movements of international scope, the most recent theories and facts, standardized methods and the international organization of studies and research. It will include a general section wherein all branches of knowledge may be represented, a number of national chairs devoted to the study of the different nations, and placed under the direct patronage of their respective governments, and a cycle of courses on international organizations and the League of Nations.

vii   *Principles*

The International University is independent of any special doctrine. The broadest spirit of tolerance prevails in the relations between its Staff, Students, and Associates.

viii   *Languages*

The recognized languages of the International University shall be French and English selected as being the official languages of the League of Nations, but every Professor or Lecturer shall be entitled to lecture in any other language provided it be of wide international use.

ix   *Administrative Seat and Premises*

The International University has its administrative seat at the International Center founded in Brussels by the Union of International Associations. An agreement shall be entered upon for placing at the disposal of the International University the scientific institutions of this center: Offices, Institutes, Laboratories and collections of the International Museum, of the International Library and of the International Bibliographical Institute.

x   *University Life*

Measures shall be taken by the Council of the University in co-operation with the Students' International Federation in order to secure the best conditions of social intercourse, comfort, welfare and cost for the organization of University life. Special facilities shall be provided for the study of modern languages.

77

XI   *Sessions. University Tours*

The International University shall organize sessions varying in length according to circumstances. It shall also organize complementary University tours with the help of the several associated Universities.

XII   *Finance*

The sources of revenue of the I. U. shall consist of:

1] Subscriptions, contributions and fees paid by the collective and individual members of the I. U.
2] Grants from the various states, public authorities and corporations, the League of Nations, the responsible national and international associations.
3] Private endowments and grants.
4] Any other source compatible with the aims of the institution.

The budget of the I.U. is drawn up annually by the Executive Committee; the annual balance sheet is submitted by the Executive Committee to the approval of the Committee.

XIII   *Revision of Statute*

The present Statute shall be revised within two calendar years by a general assembly summoned by the Executive Committee. The composition of said general assembly shall be provisionally determined by the Committee. Each of the collective members shall be represented by at least one delegate.[1]

Operating under the Statute for the first time in September, 1920, one hundred students from eleven countries attended the six-week session. They were instructed by forty-seven professors from ten nations.[2] Some of these professors temporarily filled the thirteen chairs which had been contributed by an equal number of international academic organizations. Although it was originally hoped that the six-week

78

sessions would expand into the full program envisioned, each subsequent year saw weaker and weaker participation until the entire program was disbanded in the early thirties.

The most important single factor contributing to the collapse of the International University was the constant shortage of funds. While no balance sheets are available forty years after the initial sessions, it is clear from Otlet's correspondence and speeches that the UIA was not receiving support from the four sources so hopefully listed in section xii of the Statute. In the first place, the universities and academic associations which sponsored the university were themselves in no enviable financial position, so that even sharing the financial burden was not sufficient to elicit enough funds. Second, and representing the greatest disappointment to Otlet and other university officials, was the lack of support from the League of Nations. To members of the League, and even of the Committee on Intellectual Cooperation, the scheme seemed too radical a departure from past emphasis on national institutions. It seemed too great and unnecessary a step, unwarranted before all other means of cooperation had been employed. Therefore, while conceding that the goals of the new university were probably important to international development, the League refused to offer more than the most lukewarm moral support. As noted in Chapter 3, the League preferred exchange of professors and students, and the strengthening of international studies at national universities.

The third source of revenue listed was private endowment and grants, ostensibly from large foundations, but no such aid was forthcoming. Probably an important explanation is that the university did not petition for private aid until after other sources had failed to produce. Private foundations were therefore being asked to rescue an institution already in financial trouble, already having tried to make a start, and already having failed. Such a record is not at all conducive to favorable action by large foundations, which usually shy away from ailing causes. Perhaps some personal reasons were also involved, for it cannot be said that private foundations looked askance at the principles of international higher education. As we shall see, it was the Rockefeller Foundation which initially and continually endowed the Graduate Institute of International Studies in Geneva, only seven years after the Brussels International University pilot project first opened its lecture halls, and years before that project was disbanded.

The preamble sets forth the sponsoring organizations, significantly including the two large international student federations and a small number of universities and academic associations. The complete list of original sponsors is not available. As the university was an academic institution, it was naturally crucial that other academic institutions and students recognize it as a legitimate and respected addition. There is no better way to assure that respect than to invite and secure student organizations and universities as primary sponsors of the new university, with a voice in its administration and policy. The shrewdness and significance of gathering such support was overshadowed by the lack of financial viability, so that the project failed even with academic backing. In more recent years, as national universities have developed an increasing number and variety of international study programs, they have been hesitant to recognize the need for an international university, since such recognition concedes the inadequacy of national programs. In the early 1920's, when few national programs of international study existed, this problem did not arise, so that academic approval was not so difficult to secure.

But there was a fear among educators and politicians alike that a new and dangerous internationalism would result from an international university. Such thinking seems to have been the central point of opposition to the experiment, not only in the League but within the academic community.

People wanted international understanding without an international framework. Much concern was expressed over the decline of national authority and possible blurring of lines delineating national spheres of influence.

When Otlet brought the draft Statute to the UIA for approval in 1920, many initially questioned his plan as a scheme for internationalism and utopianism. The uneasiness was best captured by the Portuguese representative: "It is necessary," he insisted, "not to intercede in the development of each country according to its abilities and national qualities. We must not want to create a purely international organ which will produce absolutely nothing. It is necessary that each country be left with its own characteristics, and to use those qualities well to cooperate toward certain common goals." [3]

It was only after the careful assurance that no invasion of national authority was implied that approval was given by the UIA. In 1952, Alexander Marc quoted Otlet as having said: "As it is not responsible for all aspects of the intellectual training of its students, the international university has no need to be all-sided. Its existence presupposes that of other universities. It will not concern itself with establishment of faculties on the traditional lines." [4] Such assurances that the new university would not compete with national universities were necessary to win support.

Even though Otlet insisted that the new university would be nothing more than a supplement to national education, the curriculum which he outlined, and which was easily accepted, seemed to contain much duplication of traditional courses. The four areas of curriculum were in the field of general studies, languages, and literature. The first included agriculture, urban development, history, pure sciences, philosophy, social and economic sciences, and other subjects commonly found elsewhere at least in name. At the new university, however, the emphasis was to be on comparison and synthesis, so, it was argued, there was a substantive difference in the course material itself. The two other categories were unlike the programs included in the national universities of the time. Comparative National Studies, with chairs sponsored by national governments, were anticipated in the Statute and not expanded in explanatory literature. Studies of International Questions were to include lectures on international law, war and peace, international politics, and the aims and operations of the League of Nations. Again, the purpose of all lectures was the discussion of the international nature and role of each of the specific subjects, and the search for common points among different national outlooks. This was the goal of the university.

In addition to assurances of national sovereignty, one other change was made in Otlet's draft Statute, giving further indication of the fear of offending anyone which overshadowed much of the then-current thinking. The final draft of section 1 includes a reference to "a proportion of students" who would study at the university. Originally, the term was "an elite of students," changed because those who were not admitted would feel insulted and perhaps fail to support the university. While not a really important change of wording, it provides insight into the worries of the age.

Five years later, Paul Otlet was still campaigning for his Brussels experiment, even though it was a losing proposition. Speaking at the first Biennial Conference of the World Federation of Education Associations in Edinburgh, he explained again his hopes and the structure of the desired university. He mentioned the international institute of Tagore and the law academy in The Hague. There were, he pointed out, similar international efforts at a Jewish University of Jerusalem, "which is very international"; at the Oriental University of Moscow, and the World University in Vienna. "All these facts," he implored, "clearly show how necessary it is, at the present moment, to establish a Central Institution, a World University, which should be in a position to co-ordinate all intellectual activities and enhance their efficiency." [5] In a final call to action, Otlet charged that "as the League of Nations are not intending to create an international university, it is the duty of International Associations now" to do so. His call went unheeded, support was not forthcoming, and Paul Otlet left Edinburgh knowing that the university would not survive. It did not.

According to the official 1962 catalogue of the Graduate Institute of International Studies in Geneva, the purpose of the Institute is "to maintain . . . a center for the study of contemporary international questions from the judicial, political, and economic points of view," and, "It entertains no preconceived doctrine, national or international, and it scrupulously abstains from any propaganda. It aspires to contribute to international solidarity solely by encouraging impartial observation and respect for facts and ideas." With these goals in mind, Professors William E. Rappard and Paul Mantoux established the Institute in 1927, and it has grown steadily stronger and more respected since then.

Study at the Institute is correlated with course work at the University of Geneva, so that Institute students take such subjects as philosophy, economic history, political economy, and even international relations at the University of Geneva. Some of these courses, while offered at the University, are taught by permanent faculty members of the Institute. A sample of seminars and lectures offered at the Institute includes History and International Politics, War and Politics, Foreign Policy of the Soviet Union, The Dilemmas of Modern Democracy, The Foreign Policy of Bismarck, and others in the general category of History and International Politics. Four other categories include courses in International Economics, International Law, International Organizations and Institutions, and Problems of Economic Development. Full-time students work for either a *licence ès science politique* or a *doctorat ès science politique*, granted after a stipulated amount of study, writing, and successful completion of examinations.

83

The purpose of the Institute is further described in the limitation placed on the curriculum. "The aim is not to cover in one or in a cycle of two or more years the whole field of international relations, but to study with care certain subjects chosen in such a manner as to throw light upon the general problems of international relations, while making the best possible use of the special resources of Geneva." Students come with a thorough background in law, political science, economics or modern history, having already earned at least one university diploma elsewhere. At the Institute, specialization in international political and economic questions is immediate and complete, with the exception of some required courses from the University of Geneva. Heavy emphasis is placed on personal research and writing while at the Institute.

The Institute was originally placed in Geneva to be close to the operations and resources of the League of Nations and the International Labor Organization. The League is gone, replaced by the European Headquarters of the United Nations, no less a source of material and example. Doctoral students have access to the library of the United Nations, ILO and League archives, as well as the libraries of the University of Geneva, and the Institute's own fifty thousand volumes of material directly related to international questions. The advantages of Geneva as a site are clear. Just as location was tied to the League of Nations, so too were the languages chosen, English and French, the official languages of the League. But to accommodate a greater variety of students, theses were and are acceptable in Italian or German as well. The location, the connection with the League and with another university, the choice of language, the orientation of the curriculum—all of these exemplify the model institution planned and hoped for by so many others. The Institute has existed since 1927, so that it is well to ask not only how it sustains itself, but also in what ways it can be considered lacking, in what sense even this Institute is not yet an international university.

The new Institute has been financially supported by grants from the Rockefeller Foundation, which has given continuous aid for well over a quarter of a century after the first session in 1927. Some costs are shifted to the University of Geneva, which pays for its own courses, even if taken by Institute students. There are independent library facilities available without any expenditure on the part of the Institute, whose collection would certainly be inadequate without the libraries of the League and UN. A number of professors are visitors on sabbatical, further defraying expenditures to the home universities of the visitors. Since it started operation, the Institute has secured annual budget authorizations from the Canton of Geneva and the Swiss Confederation, and in 1957 the Ford Foundation awarded the Institute a large grant. In addition to these sources, the catalogue reports that "la Foundation pour l'étude des relations internationales en Suisse" contributes regularly. That private foundation was established in 1957 and is maintained by private grants.

This financial picture very closely fits the often proposed combination of national government support, aid from private foundations, and the sharing of costs with other institutions by using their facilities and inviting their professors on sabbatical leave. Although the Institute provides some scholarships, most students pay tuition fees to the University of Geneva as well as to the Institute. In 1962, each student paid one hundred Swiss francs (about $28) per semester to the University and another one hundred and fifteen francs to the Institute. Compared to other sources, tuitions amount to a very small portion of total revenue and so are relatively unimportant. The fact that tuitions are paid, but scholarships provided, only rounds out the details of this prototype of most models of an international university. Why, then, has activity in this field continued long after the establishment of the Institute?

The answer lies in three limitations imposed on the Institute by its own administration. The first of these is a limitation on course material covered as part of the Institute curriculum. Connected with it is a restriction on the number of students admitted for study, never exceeding one hundred and fifty, not counting auditors who sit in on lectures but cannot participate in seminars. Also intimately related to the curricular limitations is a rather narrow scope of research. Although these limitations might be explained as a necessity in order to remain within a certain budget, a high administrative official of the Institute commented privately that there is no desire or intention to expand operations; that the site and scope of the Institute are considered proper and not in need of revision, and that financial support is not the central issue when talk of expansion arises.

As described above, the Institute curriculum touches five aspects of international relations. By comparing the courses offered with some of the proposed curricula printed elsewhere, it becomes obvious that many have wanted a much more exhaustive examination of the problems of international life. By 1962, for example, the Institute offered only one lecture and one seminar on economic development, and from the titles they were not theoretical courses. The lecture dealt with Southeast Asia, the seminar with all of Asia and Africa. But not only depth is at issue. Almost every post-World War II program has requested a much wider range of subjects in the social sciences, and most insisted on a number of courses in the physical and natural sciences as well.

There is no research in the physical sciences undertaken at the Institute, so that the many desires for such work cannot be met there. Further, the research projects in the social sciences are extremely limited in number, and, while not unimportant by any means, are not of the kind suggested in many other proposals. The 1962 catalogue lists these research projects: "a digest of decisions and documents of the written and oral proceedings of the Permanent Court of International Justice, and of the International Court of Justice . . . a planned series of studies on multilateral diplo-macy . . . [including] some of the military problems con-nected with the study of international relations . . . [and] a programme of research and publications on international social history." The scope of work does not encompass a great number of social, political, and economic problems, such as those of conflict resolution, includes none of the five top-priority concerns listed by the UNESCO Committee under Robert Angell, and few of the desired areas of re-search proposed by many other groups. The Institute is not, therefore, the answer to the need for international research voiced by many since 1927.

Perhaps a less important drawback than the content of the curricular and research programs is the small number of students and faculty at the Institute. Most supporters of international higher education have envisioned an operation including several thousand students, so that a large number of people might be touched by the atmosphere and opportu-nity of the international university. It has been argued that, to be effective, the university must reach as many as pos-sible. Some might feel that the few educated at the Graduate Institute do not constitute a group large enough to affect significantly the international situation, even though the work done at the Institute is in general of excellent qual-ity.

Although the Institute has a faculty of diverse national origin, it is predominantly European, with one or two Amer-icans and Asians. The same is true of the student body, more substantially American, although in no sense is the Institute American. But no attempt is made to balance nationalities, regions, or ideologies artificially anywhere in the Institute. Students and faculty have been there from every region, but not all at once. The fact that the Institute is largely Euro-pean might be enough to make some internationalists insist that the Institute is not international in the sense of main-taining and expressing *all* points of view. In short, the simple possibility of expression and attendance by all is no substitute for the actual presence and articulation of all important doctrines.

These, then, are four reasons why an Institute as flourishing and as seemingly exemplary of so many other proposals as the Graduate Institute of International Studies has not satisfied many who still favor strong steps toward international higher education. While recognizing that the Institute does excellent and important work, and that it is undoubtedly one of the most international centers of learning in the world, it still cannot be cited as the culmination of the effort for a world university. The narrowness of its curriculum, with a correspondingly limited research program, falls far short of programs detailed elsewhere. The small scale of operation further restrains the effect which the program could have, since it restricts greatly the number of people brought together and the total number exposed to the international atmosphere. Finally, questions could be raised as to the internationality of the Institute itself. Efforts toward an international university have, therefore, continued long after the Institute was established.

The great flurry of activity immediately following World War II took place almost entirely within the confines of UNESCO. If other groups similar to the war veterans in Rome desired an international university, they did not contact UNESCO or anyone else with any real proposal. UNESCO documents refer to requests for study of international higher education received by the preparatory commission in 1945, but no record of any actual proposal made by an outside group appears, except for the Rome group discussed in the previous chapter.

In February, 1949, a rather unusual project in international education was launched by a group of radio officials meeting in Paris. At first, eleven nations joined to sponsor the International Radio University. Coordinated from Paris under the presidency of Theodore Fleischman, radio lectures approximately ten minutes long were taped in, and distributed to, various participating countries. Where necessary, translations were made and the lecture rebroadcast over many radio stations. Special emphasis in the circulating lectures was to be placed on "representative great men," and through these broadcasts to the general public international knowledge and understanding were to be fostered. By 1959, national membership had grown to thirty. An administrative council meets every other year to decide policy.

As discussed in the previous chapter, UNESCO, ECOSOC, and the UN itself were gathering opinions from the world's social scientists, physical scientists, and other scholars. An organized report for a United Nations Institute of the Human Sciences was submitted by the Society for the Psychological Study of Social Issues, as requested by the UN. While this activity was going on, and as far back as 1943, the International Association of University Professors and Lecturers (IAUPL) was privately considering an international university, and, after the war, an International Institute of the Social Sciences. A detailed preliminary report was adopted in Basel at the 1949 Conference of the IAUPL. A summation of the report and an analysis of its motivation was printed in the Autumn, 1951, volume of the *International Social Science Bulletin of UNESCO*, written by the two British members of the IAUPL, T. S. Simey and F. T. H. Fletcher, referred to in Chapter 1. Simey had been a member of the UNESCO board of experts which met under Robert Angell earlier in the same year to discuss the International Social Science Research Center.

The authors defended the necessity for international social science research and education by declaring that it would be fallacious

to suppose that the work carried out by national institutions can ultimately be relied upon to solve international problems by a kind of automatic process, provided that a sufficient interval of time is allowed to elapse, and the impatience is adequately curbed of the person who wishes to see energetic attempts made by social scientists to attack international problems forthwith. Such projects as the study of barriers to effective communications at international conferences, or the degree to which the ordinary citizen throughout the world identifies himself with the activities of such bodies as ILO and WHO can hardly be expected to emerge as research assignments accepted by any national agency equipped with adequate means to deal with them, as well as a sufficiently clear understanding of their nature and urgency. Moreover, it is extremely unlikely that such problems can be tackled effectively with tools borrowed, as it were, from the stock created for other purposes, such as market research, the treatment of delinquency, or the maintenance of industrial morale. All the techniques so far employed are relevant in some degree, as they are designed to assist the processes of changing human behavior; where the importance of solving international problems, however, is of such a high order that the very future of our race may depend upon it, the conclusion can only be that special skills and techniques must be invented if there is to be the remotest chance of attaining objectives whose magnitude and complexity are both of the highest possible order.[6]

Simey and Fletcher write that the IAUPL originally favored an international university, but as "idealism flagged" in 1947, emphasis was placed on the more modest International Institute as a possible nucleus for further expansion. But even at the Institute, great stress would initially be laid on training young social scientists to think in terms of international relations and contexts. "It is only when there is a general awareness of the need for fundamental research in the international field, when the 'points of entry' which can be exploited for research purposes are fairly clearly understood, and lastly when an adequate number of young social scientists with training in the methods of international communication and teamwork is available, that a fully developed research program can be attempted." [7]

After presenting the justification and purpose for an international institute, the authors described a possible structure for it, taken from the report approved by the IAUPL in Basel. About fifty students would take part in the two-year program. First-year students, all at the graduate level, would be "fellows in training," and would study international relations. The best of these would continue for a second year as "research fellows," putting to practical use in research the methods and information derived from their academic background. All programs would be carried out in English and French, although operating experience might suggest other languages to be acceptable for daily use.

The institute would be located in a small, governmentally stable, and nonoppressive country, probably Switzerland. Warning against placing the institute in a politically inappropriate spot, the authors suggested that "a world power, however well intentioned it may be, unconsciously exerts by its very size and prestige a powerful influence upon all institutions set up within its borders." [8] By the same argument, all self-governing territories of Great Britain or France were ruled out as sites, because of strong "home" influence. The point has come up in a different context, when it was argued that no national university can possibly escape national perspectives consistently pervading all teaching of international relations.

The administrative organization of the institute would be similar to that frequently proposed elsewhere. A council or governing board would be appointed by the various sponsoring organizations. This board of eighteen men would decide principles and general policy. It would appoint a five-man executive board to insure proper administration of the general policies. Below the executive board would be the principal, or rector, then a vice-principal, and finally the faculty, or group leaders, directly conducting the research and classroom work.

The cost of paying the administrative agents and operating the institute as described was estimated at $500,000 per year. These funds would be solicited from private foundations and technical assistance funds. Fellowships and scholarships might come from national universities, foundations, or national commissions to UNESCO, and costs of faculty might be partially defrayed by attracting staff on sabbatical leave. The report stressed the importance of rapid, if not immediate, financial independence from any government or association of governments, so that political pressures on the institute could be kept to a minimum.

In order systematically to gain support for a world university, a number of people from Europe and the United States met in Zurich in 1953 to form the International Society for the Establishment of a World University, with headquarters in Stuttgart. The group began by circulating the idea to friends and professional academic colleagues, cultivating the approval of a German botanist, an American philosophy professor, an Indian psychologist—a number of isolated responses. Several outstanding figures responded favorably when informed of work for a world university, including Albert Schweitzer, Carl Burckhardt, and Max Huber. Letters of commendation and support were received from university directors, professors, and scholars from Japan, India, the United States, and other countries. Neither the Soviet Union nor any nation of Eastern Europe responded.

In an unpublished draft proposal in May, 1958, the Society detailed its position and its requests. The plan arose "from the awareness that all, and particularly the political and economic endeavors toward peaceful cooperation among the nations can be truly successful only if the essential condition of mutual trust is created and maintained by intellectual and spiritual forces." Because of the complicated interdependence among nations, "a university that would be limited to one continent would not meet the requirements of our time."

The major task of the new university would be the training of young people "to think and act in terms of global interrelations." All students would have completed professional or academic training at their national universities, and hopefully would be in positions of political responsibility after leaving the world university. In keeping with the desired international emphasis, all subjects would be treated "with a view to their world-wide significance." The curriculum briefly outlined in the proposal covers twenty-three fields, from the mass media to health, nutrition, and traffic; from the history of the world and its religions and literature to international law, economics, and "Problems of Social Order." Expanding the theme of the International Radio University, the Society would present to students "the Lives and Achievements of the Benefactors of Humanity." Research carried out at the university would be designed to coordinate and evaluate research undertaken elsewhere, and would be "dedicated, in a synthesis of science and humanity . . . to the solution of burning questions in all fields of human activity." Research faculty would attend for approximately six months, although a more permanent staff would insure proper continuity.

The report called for a gradual building up of the world university in a location to be decided by an international congress. Instruction would be offered in "the main languages of the world," and, repeating the plan of the League of Nations, all degrees offered should be recognized in all nations. More importantly, the Society began the process of cultivating support among students and academicians throughout the world. Representatives of student organizations from India and Latin America wrote and spoke favorably at student congresses. It is this kind of support which is ultimately the most potent influence for the establishment of an international university.

Culminating seven years of preparatory activity, the Society launched a pilot project summer session world university in 1960. Sixty graduate students attended the series of lectures, held in Strasbourg, where the problems of hunger, East-West relations, and "man and the law of man" were discussed. Deeming the first session a success, the Society established permanent headquarters at The Hague, where another summer session similar to the first was conducted in 1961. Students and faculty were selected by the secretariat of the Executive Committee of the International Society. Professor E. deVries was chosen rector, and by 1963 the project had expanded its curriculum to full-year operation and included a wider range of topics in the social sciences, among them international administration. Although still small and unsure of survival, it seems to have taken root.

Perhaps because of the publicity efforts of the Society, and perhaps because it became apparent that UNESCO was not going to take the initiative in this field, every year since 1958 has seen at least one detailed proposal for a world university, and at least three other pilot projects have been established. A larger portion of this later activity has occurred in the United States, Western Europe accounting for almost all of the remainder.

While the Stuttgart-centered Society was gathering international academic comment on its program, a nine-member Committee for a United Nations University was working toward similar ends in the United States. The Committee was a part of the Federation of American Scientists and printed its own "Proposal to Study the Founding of a United Nations University" in July, 1958, two months after the Society's unpublished announcement appeared. Similar to the Society in that it circulated its proposal to over five hundred educators, the FAS was much more subdued in its analysis of the actual programs and operations of such a university. As the title suggests, the FAS sought to initiate a formal study of the feasibility of a United Nations University. Its own report was therefore limited to a statement of need for an international university, a request for further study, and an admittedly tentative set of solutions to practical problems, presented more as points of discussion than as a definite program. The Committee proclaimed that "the time is overripe for a major co-operative effort to seek out all possible means of reducing international tensions, to discover ways of reconciling conflicting ideologies, and to build those international institutions which will be recognized to insure a just and peaceful world. A United Nations University could perform a central function in this task."

As contemplated by the FAS Committee, the university would educate simultaneously one thousand to ten thousand students, operating at first on a small scale until, over a period of years, financial and academic support would mount to permit expansion to full graduate operations as "a large university embracing all intellectual fields with a faculty and student body chosen to be representative of the entire world." Research in all fields would be of equal importance with training, and all research would be planned by the faculty. Faculty and students of highest caliber would be chosen within a broad national quota.

The university should be administered as an entirely self-governing operation, keeping outside political pressures to a minimum. All curricular policy would be formulated by a Faculty Senate, which would also direct the admission of students, appointments of faculty, and allocation of funds among the different "categories of expenditure." Initially, there might be an organizing Council "appointed by the member nations," including representatives of the UN and its specialized agencies. A Council-appointed executive group would select key administrators and faculty and, after a preparatory Faculty Senate convention, it would assume the responsibilities ascribed to it. The organizing Council might then be retained strictly in an advisory capacity.

Seeming to repeat the recommendations of the UNESCO Committee of 1951, the FAS envisioned a

95

series of single-problem research centers around the world, connected with and coordinated by the UN University itself. Each institute would work on problems of the area in which it was located, tackling research assignments one problem at a time and calling upon the research personnel necessary to probe the question. The central university would conduct some research, but would be mainly the center of training and curricular study in the natural sciences, social sciences, and humanities. In each field the UN University would "excel in areas that bear on international relations," and would not attempt to be eminent in all aspects of all academic fields. Defending and placing in perspective the desire to seek common elements among various cultures and ideologies, the Committee concluded its remarks on curriculum by pointing out that "the enlightened internationalist has no wish to see all men a common shade of gray, nor does he wish to enjoy variety at the price of poverty, ignorance, disease and misery."

The university would operate bilingually, probably selected from English, Russian, Spanish, Chinese, or French, the five most frequently spoken languages of the world. English and Russian might be the two official languages and would be learned as soon as possible by all students. But to permit as wide a policy of admissions as possible, beginning lectures might be offered with translations into all five languages with discussion groups in each language. In more advanced courses, or when translation was not feasible, Russian and English would be used.

Even though Switzerland was the "obvious choice" for location, other unspecified possibilities were recognized. Among the criteria for site selection were the language of the host country, possibilities of internationalizing the chosen territory, and the political stability and neutrality of the host nation. The branch institutes would be in different regions of the world.

The whole operation would require an estimated yearly

budget of $10,000,000 to $100,000,000. In a sober and not overly optimistic account of four possible sources of revenue, the report includes tuitions, private foundations, national governments, and the United Nations. Exploring the negative aspects of each, the Committee warned that excessive reliance on tuitions would restrict admission to wealthier students, and limit participation of vast numbers of otherwise qualified Asians, Africans, and Latins. The Committee also recognized that both UNESCO and the UN have overburdened budgets, so that substantive support would probably not be forthcoming. Further, private foundations might hesitate to assist such an experimental project unless it were assured of other simultaneous backing. Finally, reliance on national governments for financial support would open the university to political pressures, which might be minimized by securing appropriations for several years consecutively. Even this measure was recognized as weak and probably unacceptable to national governments, so that financing was candidly called "obviously the most difficult problem in founding the UN University." Still, the FAS optimistically hoped that "the people of the world can be persuaded that extravagant expenditures for war are out of balance compared to constructive enterprises directed toward peace."

The completed report was sent to some five hundred educators, diplomats, and UNESCO officials. The response was "quite encouraging." Of the more than one hundred replies, over 75 per cent were favorable. The Committee reports that university professors were "by far the most favorably inclined," while university administrators tended to be more conservative in their reactions.

In early 1958, an assistant dean of the Newark College of Engineering, Dr. Max Bedrosian, and Professor Paul Obler of the English Department of Drew University collaborated to compose "A Proposal to Extend International Understanding Through Education," by the establishment of a series of United Nations University Centers. The objectives

THE IDEA OF A WORLD UNIVERSITY

of the Centers were to provide students with international contacts and fresh perspectives, "to inculcate wider appreciation and more inclusive loyalties . . . while not ignoring the significance of particular national heritages, and to provide training for future UN ambassadors and other international civil servants." [9]

The centers would be in politically neutral states, would be administered by UNESCO, and financed by the UN. Students would be chosen by competitive examinations administered in each participating nation, but a quota system based on college-age population would provide general guide lines for admissions. Faculty would be selected in a two-stage process, applications first screened by the national committee of the country in which the applicant teaches, and finally by an international selection committee which would make final appointments. Courses of study would embrace medicine, engineering, and agriculture, as well as a complete graduate school based on the liberal arts program, "essentially the same as that found in any fine liberal arts institution in the U. S.," the difference being that the international atmosphere of the centers would place all subject matter in a new light and "engender a supra-national emphasis."

Bedrosian and Obler, like many other proponents of international higher education discussed in this chapter, sent their proposal to the Department of Education of UNESCO, which acknowledged receipt and filed the report with others of its kind. It took no action, and because Bedrosian and Obler did not follow up elsewhere, nothing developed from the work done.

A more active group also addressing UNESCO was the Inter-National University Foundation, with headquarters in New York. Headed by Dr. Karl J. Ewerts, the group had tried unsuccessfully to secure private foundation support for the construction of an international university on Ellis Island, at the time the Island ceased its function as a receiving point for immigrants to the United States. The university would provide training for international service and for "responsible leadership" by offering courses in diplomatic service and international administration, international business and finance, and advanced studies of international problems, all leading to master's degrees or doctorates in international affairs.

Students and faculty would be selected in the same fashion as that described by Bedrosian and Obler, through a two-stage operation of initial national screening and final selection by the university. A quota system would distribute students according to the population of their nations, except the United States, which, as host country, would receive representation of 20 per cent of the student body. In the above comments, Ewerts' plan sounds like most others. He belies his fundamental support for the international exchange of ideas, however, when he insists that Eastern European nations and other Communist countries be represented only by exile or refugee students and faculty. Only those nations will be recognized as welcome participants which "have proved their firm adherence to human principles of life. . . ." Instantly the project becomes part of the cold war and must be discounted as an effort toward truly international, intercultural, and interideological academic confrontation.

Eugene Staley, a Stanford Research Institute economist, objected to Ewerts' "Free University of the West," referring to it as "a very questionable idea" in relation to Staley's own proposal for a United Nations University to be completely international in scope and presentation, with campuses and research institutes in different regions of the world.[10] Staley's UN University would focus on postgraduate education, with a possibility of special teacher-training institutes in Africa (Addis Ababa) and other emerging areas. The central motivation for the university would be the addition of "a new dimension of citizenship and loyalty—that to the world community," better to cope with and support modern international interrelationships.

The expected curriculum corresponds closely to the one presented by the FAS committee over two years before Staley wrote his own proposal in October, 1960. Ultimately, the university would embrace "all the major fields of advanced research and advanced teaching and learning." The natural sciences would be included to "provide a unifying area of agreement," the same phrase as that used by the FAS. Such applied sciences as engineering, medicine, and agriculture would be pursued at related research institutes. The humanities and the social sciences would gain from synthesis developing from academic interactions. One of the research centers would be a "World Institute of Social Technology," studying the whole gamut of political and socioeconomic problems of the international order.

Staley preferred UN or UNESCO sponsorship, first because he felt that international sponsorship would reduce political pressures, and because such backing would accord important prestige to the university, attracting faculty and students. Freely admitting that the UN University would constitute competition for national institutions, Staley countered the point by noting that every well-respected university in the world is overcrowded, and that new facilities are needed, so that the new university would help to alleviate the problem. Another step to reduce political interference would be to "confine recruitment of faculty and other key operations to men of learning rather than politicians."

Staley directly discussed two other practical problems, language and finance. He was impressed by the bilingual, sometimes trilingual operations of the Graduate Institute of International Studies, where he himself had been both student and visiting faculty lecturer. Experimentation might include computerized translating machines and even "one of the constructed languages which has the advantage of great regularity and ease of learning." In any event, the university would be a center for research in communication barriers, so that results of the research could be applied to university operations themselves.

Revenue sources should as soon as possible be independent of governments. The UN might supply funds obtained from international taxation on such new developments as space travel and communication and the uses of ocean and polar resources. As these and similar fields expand, revenues for the university might be assured. As another, more immediate source of funds, national governments might contribute some small fixed percentage of their national defense budgets or gross national products. A tax of one-tenth of 1 per cent on the first would yield about $100,000,000 a year, the same amount as that produced by a one-hundredth of 1 per cent tax on gross national product. But, to avoid political pressure, major reliance should fall upon the new UN taxes as soon as possible. "It would be fitting," Staley concluded, "to devote the first portions of such revenues, derived from the peaceful achievements of science, to the upbuilding of a world university system."

Former Assistant Secretary-General of the UN Henri Laugier has on many occasions [11] called for new international or regional educational centers as tools for the effective transfer of the knowledge and technology of the more developed nations to the newly created nations of Africa and the emerging nations of Asia and Latin America. Objecting to Patrice Lumumba University in Moscow, and a similar institute for African students in Peking as centers for "the rapid acceleration of the transfer of intellectual equipment," Laugier called for a university international in faculty, administration, financing, teaching methods, and all other aspects, as well as in student participation. By developing and using teaching methods specifically designed to transfer the intellectual heritage of the modern world to those now advancing into it, the international university and its regional centers tailored to regional needs would be a "source of great inspiration" to national universities developing in the newer nations. Although he has written little on the subject compared to his interest in it, Laugier is one of the staunchest proponents of international higher education, and has consistently favored its establishment since the end of World War II.

In early 1960, a small group of New York area educators met, under the chairmanship of the late William Heard Kilpatrick, to found the Committee for the Promotion of an International University in America.[12] Membership rapidly expanded among educators and came to include U. S. Senator Jacob Javits and a wide circle of influential persons. By early 1961, the Committee and its consultant, Matta Akrawi, had written a seventeen-page unpublished description of the motivation and possible organization for such a university, and had circulated the program for comment among political and educational leaders in the United States and UNESCO.

The university would be entirely devoted to the study and possible resolution of cultural, political, and economic conflicts of interest on the international level. In general, it would prepare its graduates for some kind of international career. "It will seek, through its studies, activities, and general atmosphere, to clarify the idea of peace, to discover the conditions under which a peaceful world can exist, and to cultivate an attitude of mind and spirit oriented toward peace." An international atmosphere would be fostered by an international representation among faculty, students, and administrative staff at all levels, selected because of achievement, independence of character, and within a broad geographical quota. Furthermore, the architecture of the buildings, as well as the extracurricular activities provided, would reflect the international character of the institution.

Although the university would be politically independent of the UN and all governments, it would cooperate with those bodies by undertaking internationally significant research assignments, surveys, and other academic services. In return, the university would obtain at least a part of its operating budget, as well as the use of library and other academic facilities from governments, the UN, and its specialized agencies.

The curriculum is carefully designed to achieve the goals of the university. Besides the clarification of the peace question, such areas as the evolution and nature of modern national and international societies would be explored. Confrontation of cultures and ideologies is deemed valuable to develop understanding and possibly "integrative action." To pursue these aims, the curriculum is divided into four general categories. The "problem approach courses" "are designed to encourage thinking on a world scale with the interest of the international community in view." As the title suggests, sophisticated discussions of current international disputes and differences, such as economic development techniques, international labor standards, and war, would dominate this category. "It is thought that courses of this sort . . . should be among the first to be offered by the university. They probably constitute the best illustration of the basic contribution of an international university to the scientific study of world problems."

General survey courses would provide background for the problem courses, pointing up the international interrelations among nations and cultures in world history, world geography, and other appropriate fields. Related to this category, but not so directly international in thrust, would be basic disciplines, such as psychology, literature, business and finance, economics, and even some history and regional geography. Finally, there would be area study courses, in which concentrated attention would focus on some particular cultural and/or geographic region, including all political, economic and cultural descriptions necessary to "present" the area to the student. Students could elect to specialize in one aspect of an area, for instance, economics, but

103

would not specialize in all aspects of an area at once. Therefore, there would be considerable interrelation between area study courses and those in other categories.

The languages of instruction would be English and French, but some others could be used "if enough demand exists for it." Any student specializing in an area would be required to learn the language of that area. Instruction would be carried out by conventional means, with perhaps special emphasis on seminars and tutorials where diversity of student backgrounds seriously hampers large-class work. But the international content of each course would require fresh organization of material, so that extensive research would be needed to devise methods of including a balanced international approach to the subject matter before the university could open. This kind of curricular study might in turn suggest other courses to be offered, so that the committee report recognizes its own suggestions as purely tentative.

Among those who responded favorably to the committee study were Ahmad Ali Abadi, then Deputy Prime Minister of Iran, Chi-Pao Cheng, then acting director, UNESCO Department of Education, Frank Graham, former president of the University of North Carolina and then representative of the UN to India and Pakistan, and Chester Bowles of the U. S. Department of State. Among others who welcomed the new proposal and worked for its success were Norman Cousins and Jacques Freymond, president of the Graduate Institute of International Studies. There were, however, a number of responses which questioned the need for an international university in the light of existing international study programs and the great practical considerations involved.

Besides adding new individuals to those cognizant of and supporting the drive for international higher education, the IUA committee was the only group to recognize explicitly the problem of course organization to insure internationality. Without offering any solution, the committee referred the question to further study. This problem differs from that of simply including, for example, Marxist and capitalist interpretations of a particular economic or historical phenomenon. Rather, it asks how, perhaps, a world history course might be presented so that oriental history might smoothly and integratively be included in the more ordinary Western approach to ancient world history, which begins in Mesopotamia and moves to Greece and Rome. Both of these broad curricular problems, generally neglected in previous proposals for a world university, will be discussed in the next chapter. At the invitation of Professor Kilpatrick, chairman of the Committee, Dr. Harold Taylor carried out a feasibility study of the Committee ideas, incorporating some of them in the experiment in a world college described later in this chapter. Following Professor Kilpatrick's death in 1963, the Committee has not been active.

Very much under the influence of the IUA Committee report and the FAS proposal, as well as other earlier activity at UNESCO and the League, the Association for Commitment to World Responsibility produced three draft proposals for a United Nations University, their activity reaching a peak in 1962.[13] The interest of this student-faculty group at the University of Michigan was drawn to international higher education when it began exploring possibilities for a United Nations Service Corps, to be an international counterpart of the United States Peace Corps. Participants in the UNSC would be trained at a central institution, just as Peace Corps volunteers are trained. It was then an easy step to the more general problem of a United Nations University. Throughout 1961, ACWR conducted research, and invited faculty and foreign students to participate in exploratory seminars considering the problem of international higher education. The final draft proposal, published in February, 1962, was a mixture of original ideas and heavy reference to past work.

Reflecting the group's initial interest in international service, the ACWR proposal includes service as a function of the university, with the same priority as training and research. The curriculum proposal took the entire structure put forth in the IUA plan, and added a Faculty of Economics and Social Development, including all aspects of community planning, agricultural and industrial organization, etc. In each department within the Faculty of Economic and Social Development and the Faculty of Arts and Sciences taken from the IUA plan, research would be undertaken on appropriate problems, as planned by the Faculty Board of each department. Efforts could be made to integrate the research as closely as possible with classroom instruction. Service would be integrated into the academic program by making service with the UN or one of its specialized agencies a necessary and sufficient substitute for a purely academic doctoral thesis. The doctoral candidate would work a terminal two-year or five-year period in the field, doing whatever he is trained academically to do. He would be so placed as to be responsible for at least some degree of initiative and for the filing of periodic reports. The completion of his tour of duty to the UN would constitute the final step in the earning of a Ph.D.

ACWR recognized that a fully operating university would take years to build. The priority of curriculum again reflects the initial interest in training people to serve in an international peace corps, or UNSC. The highest priority discipline presented should be social and economic development, then arts and sciences, then, if money permits, education, law, journalism, and other professional disciplines. ACWR adopted without important change the language provisions of the FAS and IUA reports.

The UN University would be directed at six objectives other than the promotion of social and economic development. Following the approach initiated by the IUA plan, ACWR sought a contribution to the establishment of peace through clarification of definitions, requisite attitudes, and possible steps which would ameliorate world tension. The UN University would "serve as a center in the academic world for such activities not possible within the scope of traditional universities"; for example, an international library, the conduct of research similar to the International Geophysical Year; and, in general, "information gathering, appraisal and distribution." Related to the peace issue, the UN University might also train international disarmament inspection teams, a task unsuited for any national university. And finally, the UN University would "effect a confrontation" of ideology, culture, and belief.

Activity of the university would "seek out the sources and bases for differing truths about the needs and conditions of human society," and, in the light of these truths and of knowledge gained from the pursuit of the other objectives, consider the basis and nature of modern society. Overall, the university would also have "to produce persons who habitually think internationally and consider current problems from a world point of view." Such problems as location, faculty and student selection, and finance were restated largely unchanged from the FAS, IUA, and Staley reports. The ACWR proposal briefly deals with four sources of sponsorship for an international university. It could be established by national universities, as a "collective subsidiary"; it could be the result of private efforts; it could become part of the UN or UNESCO, or it could be a specialized agency of the UN. The first three alternatives are dismissed, the first as unrealistic because of the lack of enthusiasm shown for the idea among university administrators, "although many professors have been interested." The second and third are discounted because of the possibilities of political bias and pressure, and because of limited financial resources. Almost by default, then, the UN University would be a new specialized agency of the United Nations.

Describing an administrative structure quite similar to

others before it, ACWR suggests that either the UN, UNESCO, or some independent international organization call a conference of experts in education and administration to discuss the UN University. From among its own members, the conference would appoint a Governing Body of fifteen, "representing universities of fifteen countries, with due respect for adequate regional representation." The group would make detailed plans for the construction and organization of the UN University, subject to final approval of the General Conference. The Governing Body would appoint a president and key faculty and administrators, who would then appoint a lower-level staff. Each curricular department faculty would decide research and course content within the department, subject to overall coordination by the Governing Body.

ACWR used the summer of 1962 to circulate its proposal at UNESCO, the United States Department of State, and at the annual convention of the United States National Student Association. Assistant Undersecretary of State Andrew Rice gave a favorable official response. USNSA adopted a resolution supporting the UN University and pledging moral and financial support to help circulate the idea. UNESCO personnel maintained official reserve when the proposal was personally presented to them. Privately, all who saw the proposal acknowledged its value as an ideal to be approached, but most also felt that practical obstacles to financial and political independence made a UN University unfeasible. The efforts of ACWR to persuade UNESCO to adopt a formal study of the project failed.

During the summer of 1962, Norwegian educator Martin Strømnes also came to the UNESCO headquarters in Paris to lobby for an international university, to be located in Scandinavia and dedicated to Dag Hammarskjold. Armed with little more than dedication to the idea, he, too, was unsuccessful in his approach to UNESCO. That same summer, Dwight Eisenhower proposed an "international school for global understanding" to the World Confederation of Organizations of the Teaching Profession, meeting in Stockholm. Two thousand students would study world history, diplomacy, politics, international communication, and teaching, all nations participating with the understanding that "only truth and objectivity have any place in the school curriculum." The UN General Assembly would be charged with the responsibility of faculty selection, and costs would be prorated among the participating nations. Mr. Eisenhower's address was reported to have received a standing ovation.[14]

Under the direction of American Professor Harold Taylor, a pilot project for a World College was operated in the summer of 1963 on Long Island, as one phase of the then four-year-old plan by the Quakers for such an institution. The first expression favoring the establishment of a world college came in 1959, when the New York Yearly Meeting of the Religious Society of Friends concluded that a world university was both "feasible and needed." A committee of New York Quakers was set up at that time to study and promote the Friends World College. In 1960, it was authorized to solicit funds and property to be held by the Trustees of the Yearly Meeting.

By July, 1960, the Committee on a Friends World College reported to the New York Yearly Meeting, outlining those aims and programs for the college which it felt were feasible, yet consistent with the goals of the Society of Friends. The college would be "international in spirit, character and influence, with a faculty and student body consisting of people of all faiths, races, and nationalities." At the same time, it would "be and remain a *Friends* college, Quaker in spirit, character, and influence." The essential goal of the college also reveals the Quaker background, seeking to solve human problems while reflecting "the spiritual unity and community of mankind." Unlike most other proposals, this one called for a small student body, not to exceed five hundred, but numbering perhaps one hundred in the opening session. The Committee felt that any larger size would destroy the feeling of close international, interpersonal atmosphere which it considered essential to the building of understanding.

The Committee report left curriculum details to the future faculty to decide but did set general policy outlines. "Special attention should be given to the study of social processes at work in relations among peoples and nations, with emphasis on peaceful methods of settling differences." In addition to a curriculum oriented toward the social sciences and humanities, a center for research on conflict resolution would be an integral part of the college. Emphasis would be placed on independent study and research, and, of course, "a world outlook should be maintained throughout the curriculum."

Students and faculty would be drawn mainly, but not exclusively, from Quaker sources. They would be referred to the college either by their local Society of Friends, by their governments, or would be invited by the college itself. All would be expected to conduct academic work in English. The Committee was able to report a donation of ten acres of land with buildings, as a site for the college on Long Island, near New York City. The site would provide frequent and extensive use of the variety of cultural and political references of New York City, notably those of the UN. All operating costs would be met through tuitions and private endowments.

Professor Taylor was invited to conduct a pilot project during the summer of 1963, using the available campus on Long Island. Dr. Taylor did so as one phase of his study of the practical problems of establishing a world university, although his experiment had no formal relation to the Quaker religion; it was conceived as a model world college in which all religious philosophies shared equal status.

Twenty-two United Nations countries participated, each represented by one student, from North and South America, Europe, the Middle East, Africa and the Socialist Republics.[15] There were six faculty members, one each from the United States, Great Britain, India, Japan, and Kenya, including Sir Robert Watson-Watt, F.R.S., developer of radar; Amiya Chakravarty, a former associate of Gandhi and Tagore; Takeshi Ishida, political scientist from Japan; and Arthur Lall, formerly head of the Indian delegation to the Geneva disarmament negotiations. Polish, Rumanian, and Iranian personnel at the UN were among the guest lecturers. A student and a philosophy professor from the Soviet Union were invited and, although the Soviet response was favorable, arrangements could not be cleared in time to secure their presence. The same was true for a Cuban student.

Governments were asked to support their national students by paying $600 tuition plus travel to and from the college. This was done in some cases, although the College supplied scholarships for those whose governments could not (by current provisions) support them financially. All other costs of operation and upkeep, approximately $16,000 for six weeks, were provided by private donations. Students and faculty were initially invited through national missions to the U.N. The curriculum was devised by the students and faculty working together, and was centered on three issues identified by the students; the problem of world order and disarmament, ideological conflict, and the gap between the rich and poor countries. Working in seminars, research projects, and daily meetings of the whole college, supplemented with field trips to the UN, the students studied a wide variety of specific topics within the three broad categories named above. Each student carried out original research in some phase of the curriculum; each was assigned to a faculty member, who acted as guide and tutor in the student's individual work.

A final report on the operation of the project includes an

optimistic résumé from the faculty of the results of the experiment. Among other items, the report states that "the feasibility of instituting a world college and/or a university on a more complete scale was established," and that "a beginning was made in solving the problem of building an international curriculum on the basis of national cultures." Further, "the idea that an educational program designed to teach a world perspective could develop increased tolerance and understanding among nationals of widely different cultures was conclusively proven. . . . In almost every instance, changes were observable in students' attitudes toward their own national or ideological biases." [16] Most conclusively, Taylor and the faculty felt that "the experiment served its purpose, not only in demonstrating the feasibility of institutions of this kind, but in encouraging educators and others to move in this direction." Based on this success, efforts have been undertaken by the Committee on a Friends World College to establish a full four-year world college on Long Island. A Friends World Institute, forerunner of the college, which is to have seven regional centers throughout the world, received its first students in September, 1965.

It is still too early to ascertain the outcome of the Friends World College. Its auspicious beginning indicates that at least limited activity on an international academic level is possible. The students and faculty who met for the six-week experimental session comprised the most heterogeneous group ever assembled in such a project, and the reported success is a hopeful sign. But like many of the other pilot projects, the Taylor experiment was too small to be more than a prototype of a pattern of study which might be part of a much more fully developed curriculum. The experiment showed that in practice a culturally mixed academic society can develop a genuinely international curriculum. Whether or not enough money will be available to support expanded operations is another question, different in kind from matters of principle.

112

Although the Friends World College differs in certain respects from other proposals and projects, it contains several elements which are common to all suggestions for international higher education. First, there is the desire to lessen world tensions and to help insure a peaceful world where problems common to many nations could be attacked with common international effort. There are aspirations to raise the level of political responsibility and academic activity to the international plane, and the belief that traditional programs of student and faculty exchange cannot be substitutes for the international nature of the world university. Second, underlying all interest in the field is the fundamental belief that higher education can be an effective element in the shaping of attitudes and responsibilities. Emphasis has been directed toward international education because many have felt that the role of traditional universities, as the transmitter of basic societal values, makes it impossible for national universities fully and dynamically to present those ideologies and perspectives which are inimical to the roots of the society in which the university is located.

The most frequently considered practical element of a world university has been the overall curricular content. The great majority of proposals have given highest priority to the social sciences, in keeping with the prevalent concern for studies of international relations. Where scientific cooperation has been the prime motivation, social sciences have naturally assumed less importance. Other practical problems have been considered, and in some cases plausible solutions have been presented. The importance of these practical proposals lies in their indication of possible lines of action and in their potential role as tangible points of departure for further, perhaps more fruitful investigations. The work of the Federation of American Scientists, the Stuttgart-centered International Society for the Establishment of a World University, the Association for Commitment to World Responsibility, the Committee for the Promotion of an International University in America, as well as the Friends experiment and other proposals, indicate that broad backing could result from wide circulation of the idea. Until now, however, no major practical effort has been made to achieve the world university which the world admits is needed. This is partially due to lack of financial support, but more fundamental difficulties have obstructed the path toward an international university.

6

WHAT NEEDS TO BE DONE

ALTHOUGH THERE is as yet no world university in existence, time has changed the tone of the discussions about the idea. It is convenient to choose World War II as a dividing point, partly because it separates League and UNESCO activity, partly because the war seems to have resulted in certain changes of attitude concerning national institutions and international activity. There can be no definitive analysis of contemporary attitudes concerning a topic as infrequently debated as international higher education. But from the formal proceedings of the League and UNESCO, and from informal private discussions with officials of UNESCO, the International Association of Universities, and World University Service, certain patterns can be discerned. In the earliest instances immediately following World War I, Otlet and others brought the topic of an international university to two groups—the League of Nations and private academic associations. The two reacted differently, as indeed their interests were different.

The League of Nations was fundamentally designed to clear away all obstacles to the free and peaceful development of cultures, traditions, and institutions. It reflected the great faith in nationalism from before 1914, tempered by the cognition that some international coordination was necessary to avoid war. The realization, which led to the creation of the League, did not in any tangible way alter or weaken the essential belief that national institutions should be supported and allowed to mature. It was this kind of enlightened nationalism which led the League to recognize the need for international understanding, but to prefer a bolstering of national education programs to achieve that end. It was this enduring faith in national institutions and heritages, coordinated by the League, which led to the creation of the International University Information Office, a central international clearing house for information about any university in the world. The Office was designed to expedite study and travel abroad, as well as student and faculty exchange programs. In this way the League fulfilled its responsibility as international coordinator, doing all it could to stimulate international understanding and cooperation while carefully preserving the sovereignty and integrity of each nation and its institutions.

League opposition to a world university, therefore, stemmed from what it felt to be a matter of principle. While the League and the CIC were fully sympathetic with the goals of international higher education, the coordination of research and the development of international understanding as a basis of peace, the League did not find a world university compatible with the desire to maintain the primacy of national institutions. The support of an international university, it was correctly observed, would imply that national universities were unable to accomplish certain important educational tasks, and the new university would therefore bypass national institutions. It was this implication which was contrary to the principles of the League of Nations and the tenets of enlightened nationalism.

It has often been noted that the League was a passive organization, incapable of decisive action. In a sense, this is not true in educational matters, for the League did take positive steps to expedite exchanges and other programs. It could, and did, do much. But the positive actions and the organizations created were themselves passive in a fundamental way, since they were designed to allow existing national programs to function, perhaps more efficiently, and not at all to supplant those programs with any supranational activity. Because a world university of the kind proposed by Barany, Bannerjea, and others would have been a supranational project largely independent of national programs, it could not secure support. For the same reasons, Otlet never received real support from the League for his Brussels International University, nor did the Graduate Institute of International Studies. Both were more favorably viewed by academic associations, probably not because of any fundamental difference in kind between the principles of the League and those of the academic associations, but because of a difference in the degree of their application. It will be remembered that Otlet did not receive endorsement from the Union of International Associations in 1920 until he carefully explained that the International University was only a supplement to national universities, and in no way constituted a move toward internationalism, nor a deprecation of national potentials. The Graduate Institute was constituted a part of the University of Geneva, so that it was very nearly a center of international studies within a national university, therefore consistent with the desires to bolster national institutions.

Like the League, academic associations tended to reflect

117

the current enlightened nationalism in their approaches to the development of international understanding. But political pressures were not as great within the academic community. Therefore, moves toward international higher education were more readily accepted once assurances were given that the new university was not a kind of usurper of national prerogatives. This flexibility of academic associations, together with the limited nature of the Brussels experiment and the Institute, explains the support given to both of them by academic associations.

If World War I enlightened prewar nationalism by stimulating interest in international cooperation and understanding, World War II went still further in prompting modification of national sovereignty. Whereas interwar political doctrines had conceded to international bodies the right of coordination, postwar agreements allowed a much greater scope of independent authority to reside in the new international organizations, among them UNESCO. Coordination was no longer considered sufficient; national development was no longer completely trusted to solve all international problems; a basic shift in political philosophy began to afford consideration to substantive supranational actions.

Within UNESCO, international higher education was no longer discarded as contrary to political principles; CERN was supported; international research centers on social and economic development were established in Southeast Asia. The new orientation resulted in more striking manifestations in the United Nations police actions in Korea and the Middle East. Interwar desires for international understanding were complemented by postwar desires for international responsibility. Academic associations and personnel have also shifted away from former emphases on national development and share recent interests in promoting and enforcing international responsibilities. In many cases, however, they have not favored an international university as a means of promoting such responsibility, nor do they generally agree that a world university could substantially improve international understanding beyond work already done at national centers.

Since 1918, increasing attention and hope have been focused on the development of international study and other programs within national universities, and much progress in this direction has been made. Such programs have been supported to promote understanding and cooperation and, more recently, to promote responsibilities to the world community in addition to the national community. Administrators of such centers and programs, and many faculty members connected with them, believe that their programs and techniques can do all they are supposed to do. The heart of present academic opposition to world universities lies in the belief that national universities, honest in their approaches to world problems and internationalized through frequent exchanges and excellent libraries, are capable of performing the academic tasks of a world university. They do not believe that an international university could possibly add substantively to the educational process. Because of this, academic associations often view a new world university as unnecessary competition for money and outstanding faculty and students. The Federation of American Scientists and other organizations, which have circulated plans for a world university to individuals in the academic community, report a somewhat more favorable response than is forthcoming from academic associations. The FAS states that of several hundred persons contacted, nearly all faculty endorsed international higher education, whereas only about half the administrators approved the idea.

UNESCO has been somewhat more willing to acknowledge an important role for international higher education. Its support for CERN and the newly created International Institute of Educational Planning are but two instances of UNESCO reliance on supranational activity initiated to accomplish educational tasks felt to be unattainable in any national university. But UNESCO has not come to support an international university because it does not believe such an institution to be feasible. Specifically, it does not believe that adequate finances would be made available. More fundamentally, UNESCO officials have said that political pressures and the wide variety of cultural and ideological outlooks would make the international presentation of subject matter an impossible task. The last part of this chapter is devoted to a more detailed discussion of these and other practical problems related to the establishment and operation of an international university.

By the middle fifties, UNESCO had shifted its attention away from matters of higher education, focusing nearly all its educational resources and programs on primary, secondary, and adult education. Later approaches to UNESCO for support of an international university have therefore faced the problem of irrelevancy to the central part of UNESCO's educational program, as well as the constant matter of practicality. UNESCO has consistently taken the position that it is more efficient, more economical, and less disruptive to develop national institutions. Along with World University Service and the International Association of Universities, it believes that everything possible should be done to strengthen existing institutions, rather than to bypass them with an entirely new and expensive international educational experiment. Present reliance on national institutions stems from pragmatic decisions, and is motivated altogether differently from interwar preferences for national institutions. There is, in addition, a real question as to whether UNESCO, with its bureaucratic necessities and unavoidable academic conservatism (the world's academic community has been educated within the traditional university system), is the appropriate body to sponsor a world university or to do more than simply make available its communication services to those most interested. The liveliest institutions of education are those begun by the efforts of persons devoted passionately to innovation and invention, a role which is not entirely congenial to UNESCO itself.

In general, then, grounds for opposition to an international university have shifted from a conflict of principles to a question of feasibility, evidenced both in UNESCO and within the academic world. Practicality has always been an important matter, but its current position as the center of discussion indicates that the previous issues of principle have been essentially resolved in favor of international higher education. Whereas the earliest debates rarely had an opportunity to proceed beyond the issues of nationalism versus internationalism, recent discussions proceed almost immediately to problems of location, finance, etc., quickly granting the compatibility of a world university with contemporary attitudes toward national institutions and supranational activity. In this sense, the acceptance and operation of a world university is more readily attainable today than it was forty years ago. But it is still no easy matter to present academically responsible and politically acceptable programs. A great deal of research and work is still needed before a world university can become a reality.

There are seven aspects of stucture which have gained attention and need planning to complete a program for an international university. They are, (not necessarily in order of importance) language(s) to be used, location, financial support, selection of faculty, selection of students, organization of the university's administrative staff and procedure, and the content and manner of presentation of the curriculum and research. What follows in this chapter is a general discussion of some of these matters, with concrete suggestions where relevant.

Whatever the specific languages chosen for an international university, there is little question that a bilingual university can operate successfully. The University of Ottawa uses French and English, as does the Graduate Institute for International Studies in Geneva. There are countless summer study programs in Europe which conduct lectures in two languages, usually French and English, but often including German or the language of the country in which the seminar is conducted. The practicality of bilingual or even trilingual operations without extensive translation or interpretation facilities has ample precedent. At the United Nations over the past twenty years, English and French have come to be accepted as international languages without nationalistic overtones. Provided sufficient funds were available for equipment and personnel, it is possible that simultaneous translation, using individual earphones as at the United Nations, could be employed for the major lectures. In addition, the world university would be the natural location of a world translation project for translating all the major documents of each country into the language of others. The use of English and French as the basic university languages would also make as many students as possible eligible to attend the university, a consideration perhaps more important than the political aspects. French and English are widely known first and second languages, and among high-level students of political and economic relations the modern world requires knowledge of one or both languages. The same is true of the natural and physical sciences.

The question of location is a serious one. As the previous discussion has shown, the usual suggestion has been Geneva because of its neutral political status and the access to existing UN and international libraries and personnel. The late Professor Leo Szilard argued for Vienna, on the grounds that it was a neutral point between East and West. On the other hand, it is of some significance that the location be one not far removed from the vital centers of intellectual and political activity, both in terms of the vitality of the university life itself and the possibility of recruiting first-rate intellectuals to the faculty. The area of New York City has been put forward as a natural center for this reason, as have Tokyo, Paris, London, and New Delhi. A third alternative, one of growing importance when the world situation is considered, is a series of regional world colleges so that, in a sense, the world could be brought to the continental regions rather than assuming that there is a center for the world and that that center lies in the West.

The most important single factor at the outset will be the ability of the world university to find financial backing. There are six basic sources of revenue open to an international university: private foundations, endowments and bequests from individuals, the UN and its specialized agencies, particularly UNESCO, national governments, tuitions, and universities and academic associations. It is impossible to predict the reaction of any of these sources, for they depend upon the avowed purpose of the university, its administrative structure and curricular scope, the nature of university sponsorship, and the imponderables of politics. Nevertheless, some general conclusions can be reached. It is probably naïve to hope that universities and academic associations could contribute significantly to the financial support of an international university. It is a rare university which has enough money to support itself, and academic associations, particularly on the international level, are notoriously insolvent. These institutions can play some part in supporting an international university, but it is too much to expect any significant direct financial contribution from them. The most likely arrangement is one approximating the support for the United Nations Institute for Training and Research in New York and CERN in Geneva—prorated contributions by cooperating governments, plus foundation funds and gifts from individuals. In addition, many of the research projects now supported by agencies of the UN and UNESCO could be transferred to the new institution, and additional research contracts could be assigned. The idea of a tax on the proceeds of international projects or a tithing contribution from national armaments budgets could also be explored.

The importance of tuition payments in the total university budget is impossible to predict, but it should play as small a role as possible. The FAS report states that American universities in 1950 accounted for 58 per cent of all costs through tuitions. From this, the report concludes that no greater percentage of costs should be borne directly by students at a UN university, in order that the new institution would be competitive with American universities from the student's viewpoint. However, the problem of tuition competition seems to be an empty one as long as the curriculum and atmosphere of the university are substantially different from those of traditional institutions. But unless large numbers of scholarships are offered, either by the university or by national governments, UNESCO or other sources, high tuition costs do restrict attendance to the relatively more wealthy, a situation to be avoided whenever possible. The fact that most universities outside the United States operate with nominal tuition fees is an indication that this kind of budget asset is not necessarily required for the successful operation of a university. The degree of support afforded by national governments would be mainly a practical question. The example of the United Nations Institute for Training and Research is once more the most relevant instance. As of July, 1965, forty-eight nations had made contributions toward the $10,000,000 budget; twenty others had pledged; the Rockefeller Foundation had contributed $500,000 for a building; and other foundations and individuals have contributed. Wherever there are educational advantages which are clearly seen, financial support from governments will be forthcoming.

Similarly, the problem of political control is made less severe when each nation is represented but none allowed to dominate. The United Nations Institute for Training and Research Board of Trustees consists of representatives of each major world area, fourteen in number, although the Soviets and Eastern Europeans are not part of the program. A comparable arrangement would no doubt be acceptable to all countries which support the aims and principles of international higher education, and they, after all, are the ones whose contributions would be sought. In addition to these direct sources of money, academic associations, governments, and private sources might endow individual chairs within departments. A single professorship would involve a relatively small financial commitment for each academic association, but all together might spare the university a substantial expense. National governments might consider appointing such professors directly, making government participation more attractive. Such appointments could be part of the national representation discussed above in return for more general and substantial government aid. Some proposals have suggested that the teaching staff be maintained with professors on sabbatical leave, thereby shifting a large portion of the responsibility for their salaries back to the professor's home university. While this might be somewhat effective, few professors would be willing to spend their year's leave teaching rather than traveling or working solely in research. Visiting professors could undoubtedly be attracted, but not usually during sabbaticals, and therefore not usually without full costs being borne by the international university. Proper location of the university might provide a library and some research facilities, already operated by cooperating institutions in the area. The UN headquarters would be the single most beneficial associate institution in this respect. There can be no question that there is enough money available in the world to finance a $50,000,000 per year university. But a sense of urgency must develop around the idea. The critical task facing proponents of international higher education is therefore to initiate and heighten such a concern within government and academic circles, and among private foundations.

Along with financial support, the curriculum has been a frequent subject of skeptical remarks from those who doubt the feasibility of an international university. There are two general aspects of this problem: the overall emphasis and content of the curriculum, and the organization of individual courses and disciplines to insure their internationality. Whenever curriculum has been discussed in proposals for a world university, the first aspect has been addressed with no observations related to the latter, more difficult problem. The question of overall curricular content is essentially one of definition. Most proponents of an international university have stressed the social sciences, consistent with their desires to explore the differences among political and cultural spheres of influence. A different motivation would result in different curricular priorities more closely related to the new set of goals. The most promising concept in curriculum organization is one which would stress the common interest of the world's scientists and scholars in certain key questions of importance to the contemporary world—problems in oceanography, parasitology, agriculture, economic planning and development, desalinization, mass education, solution of conflict, and the study and performance of the arts of various cultures. The use of new techniques of teaching through television, communications satellites, international radio, films, etc., would give new impetus to the idea of an international curriculum. The study of sociology, for example, if carried out by comparative studies in which the scholars of many cultures collaborated, would benefit enormously by the opportunities of such an international setting.

The matter of curricular level brings together a different set of considerations. A strong case can be made that undergraduate teaching, desirable though it may be, would not be possible at an international university. Graduates from secondary schools in different parts of the world have widely different academic backgrounds, which become more similar the more years each student spends at a traditional university. This great diversity at early levels may be enough to make effective undergraduate teaching impossible, although the new experiments in Geneva with international examinations and curricula for graduates of secondary schools show promise of success in the later high school years. However, language skills of students would not be fully enough developed in the undergraduate years to expect only two languages to encompass students from all countries. The relative lack of maturity and academic experience of undergraduates would also reduce the profundity of the crosscultural confrontation, even though personally the younger students would be more impressionable and flexible than graduate and postgraduate students. These considerations suggest that the international university would preferably begin at the graduate level.

While it is possible to structure nearly any curriculum one desires for a world university, it has often been argued that it is not possible to internationalize each course or discipline to distinguish it from traditional curricula. One might agree, for instance, to teach the theory and practice of economic development, but what should be included in the course to make it international, if it is understood that an international presentation is one which reflects the approaches, interpretations, and perspectives of the major academic and/or political factions and trends? This is the fundamental problem of the international curriculum and it goes to the very roots of the successful conduct of an international university. The central issue seems to be the difficulty of identifying "a" representative of "a" culture, "an" ideology, or "a" political bloc. After placing a course in economic development on the program, one might decide to invite lecturers representing the Western point of view, the Communist point of view, and so forth. But who represents the Western point of view, and is it even sensible to talk of "a" point of view, implying a monolithic bloc?

The task of giving a satisfactory answer to these questions is simplified by looking beyond political identifications to other characteristics of professors and ideas. Political blocs divide the world along certain lines, grouping nations and their citizens into governmentally determined alliances. But there are factional divisions and alliances within academic disciplines as well. Occasionally, especially in some phases of political and economic theory and practice, academic factions closely parallel political blocs, and it makes sense to think of a representative of the bloc and the academic trend at the same time. More frequently, academic factions ally individuals from many nations and from politically opposed camps into a single school of thought, and it is misleading to seek a representative of the particular school according to political or national criteria.

The courses at an international university would be designed to reflect all the major trends and emphases which characterize the disciplines included in the general curriculum. The university would be international in a strict sense because most of the political and historical faculties would have to include representatives of many countries, and all nations would be represented within the faculty as a whole. This population in itself would create an international atmosphere of give and take. But the university would contribute to international understanding in a broader sense as well. By the very composition of each course and discipline, study at the international university would effectively disentangle each of the conflicting ideologies, bringing out unifying trends and more clearly defining those trends which divide disciplines along political and ideological lines. (This was the experience of the faculty and students in the Taylor pilot project on Long Island.) It is true, as critics of a world university often point out, that political disagreements would deeply divide some of the disciplines of the university. This should not be a criticism, for it is a positive and important characteristic of the international nature of the university, whereby ideological differences are explored and political claims made in an academic surrounding, not in the crude milieu of polemical propaganda. It is the essence of intellectual confrontation and one of the distinctive attributes of a world university which cannot be duplicated in a traditional institution.

The task of defining the trends and factions within each discipline might well be left to the relevant international academic association. A central organizing committee of the international university, perhaps named by the UNESCO Department of Education and Director General, might coordinate the curricular studies before the opening of the university. The international associations and the organizing committee might appoint a faculty to assist in designing the curriculum. Different perspectives and trends might be presented by several lecturers within the same course, or within a series of courses, each studying in detail a single approach to the subject. The former method would be the more efficient financially, and probably academically, but time and political pressures might require the latter alternative, affording more extensive coverage of each outlook.

Many proposals have stressed the idea that the individual faculty members of an international university should be internationally minded, free from ideological bias, and in general not nationalistic. These qualities have been sought because they describe what the entire university should be. These restrictions on individual professors are not only unnecessary but undesirable and contrary to the principles of the international curriculum outlined above. Each academic faction and perspective should be presented by its own exponent, and where the faction parallels national interests a nationalistic person should be on the faculty. In legal practice, impartial attorneys never plead cases; the outcome of the judicial process is evolved through the confrontation of legal adversaries convinced of the defendant's innocence or guilt. Neither should impartial professors present ideologies or other academic ideas. Full latitude of academic freedom must be the hallmark of the international university. Any attempt to restrict professors because of their beliefs or patriotism would be contrary to that freedom and would undermine the vivid confrontation which should be a part of the curriculum.

Absolutely essential to the successful operation of a new university is respect for it within the established academic community. Many intangibles elicit this respect, but a few definite qualities can be identified as important. First, the university should have excellent research facilities, including library and equipment. If not directly owned by the university, such resources should be completely available to it at all times.

The maintenance of outstanding teaching and research facilities at the new university depends upon the amount of financial support available. In the probable event of limited funds to begin with, the university should limit its total program to an appropriately small number of disciplines, but afford excellent facilities in each. Only the first-rate will attract students and professors from well-endowed, re-spected institutions. This need for academic recognition goes far beyond the old League concern that diplomas be internationally accepted. Rather, the recognition needed is one which will attract outstanding faculty, and subsequently excellent students, for reasons other than idealism. To achieve this end, something substantive and distinctive must characterize the new university in the field of research and in the matter of curricular content.

One other aspect of the organization and operation of an international university of great importance to its ultimate success is the type of sponsorship which the new institution receives. In the past, all international higher education pilot projects have been sponsored and initiated by private groups and individuals. None has become a successful, full-scale university, although the Graduate Institute of International Studies has operated on a limited scale for nearly forty years. As mentioned above, strictly private sponsorship would make it impossible for national governments to contribute to the financial support of the university. Only an internationally sponsored, planned, and operated university, executed from the beginning by respected international organizations, could win for itself recognition as a truly international endeavor. Without such recognition, the new university would have a difficult time securing assistance from private foundations.

UNESCO or UN sponsorship of one kind or another is needed to attract academic and political prestige to the university. It is needed to attract research projects and outstanding faculty. It is needed to attract financial support. It is especially needed to help secure the new university as the international symbol of cooperation which it ought to be. Sponsorship by a natural coalition of UNESCO and the international academic associations would make it possible for the international university to operate on a much larger scale than is possible with the more limited resources and prestige of a private international institution. Although many important and successful national universities are private, the necessary internationality of the new institution places it in a special context, where private resources are not of the kind needed to insure success.

The fact that an existing international body must act as sponsor of a successful international university does not mean that private individuals and groups have no role to play, or that they can do nothing until UNESCO or the UN act. On the contrary, it is the arduous and intricate task of private persons to convince national governments that an international university is not only a desirable and feasible project, but that academic and financial supporters would be forthcoming immediately and enthusiastically if formal sponsorship and initiation were undertaken by governments. UNESCO will not proceed with a project for a world university; UNESCO does not at present believe

131

it to be feasible, nor does it believe there is widespread academic support for the idea. Private groups interested in an international university should therefore direct their efforts at dispelling these notions wherever possible.

A number of specific responsibilities are included in this effort. Private groups should secure pledges of support and participation from student and faculty associations throughout the world. They should obtain pledges of financial support from as many foundations, individuals, and associations as possible, all preparatory to the foundation of world universities by the appropriate international bodies. Whenever possible, academic associations should be urged to pass resolutions favorable to a world university, perhaps agreeing to endow at least one chair as soon as the university is created. Based on these pledges of support and other considerations, it is the paramount task of private individuals to develop completely detailed and demonstrably workable solutions to the problems of location, language, administration, finance, composition and selection of faculty, and the structure of the curriculum. UNESCO and the United Nations, along with the nongovernmental organizations of each member country, can act as aids and partners in the creation of new and truly international institutions of education. A glance at the summary of proposals made during the past and present will indicate that everywhere in the world there are people who want to see in existence the kind of educational institutions which represent in reality the hope of mankind for a cooperative endeavor to solve man's problems. It is clear that our first task must be to give these proposals and these ideas a wide hearing and a vigorous support. Out of this may come the educational institutions we seek.

APPENDICES

A Existing international institutions which approximate, or might become, world universities

AT THE PRESENT time no single institution exists which can properly be called a world university—that is, an institution with a fully international curriculum of the major university disciplines of knowledge, with a student body and faculty representing every major cultural and geographical area of the world. Some are closer to the concept than others, all are limited in some measure by present circumstance.

In the following summary an effort has been made to judge the degree to which each institution approximates the concept of complete internationality, and to identify institutions which, if developed further, could become genuine world universities. For example, if the East-West Center in Hawaii were open to students and faculty from all major continental areas, including Communist China, and a curriculum were planned to include all major cultures and sciences, it would become a world center rather than an American-sponsored Asian-American institute. Or, if a series of regional world centers were established, with completely internationalized curricula in the arts and sciences, open to students and faculty of all countries, the interchange of faculty and students among them would form a global network within the world's present academic community.

On the other hand, there are institutions staffed by scholars which in structure are already world institutions, such as the Economic Development Institute of the International Bank for Reconstruction and Development, or the United Nations Institute for Training and Research, but which serve a more limited purpose than that of a world university. These are extremely valuable as examples of international structure, since they point to a form of organization—international governing bodies, financial subsidy by a variety of nations, research projects of significance to world problems, work by scholars in which graduate students may join—which could be transposed directly into the field of higher education were there sufficient interest in making such a transposition.

The first category consists of institutions, some of which are related in some way to the United Nations and are involved in research and projects, with possibilities for extension into the educational field on a larger international scale.

CERN (European Organization for Nuclear Research), Meyrin, Geneva 23, Switzerland, was founded July 1, 1953, through the cooperation of scientists and officials of thirteen European governments (Austria, Belgium, Denmark, Spain, France, Greece, Italy, Norway, the Netherlands, Germany, the United Kingdom, Sweden, and Switzerland) as a center for cooperative research in high energy physics. The center was designed to provide the necessary equipment and personnel for advanced research, equipment more expensive and complicated than any one country could easily furnish for itself. CERN provides research facilities for approximately sixty-five resident scientists from the sponsoring countries, three hundred visiting scientists, and courses enrolling five hundred and fifty students from a highly selected roster of applicants. Among other activities the center conducts a translation service for its research results, a public information service, and a monthly journal.

The administration includes a president of the international three-man governing council and an international scientific executive committee, each member of which is a practicing scientist in a particular field. Funds are supplied by the governments involved on an apportionment basis, with the larger contributions coming from France, Great Britain, and West Germany. Visiting scientists join the center on a selected basis and include persons from Canada, Brazil, Nationalist China, the United States, Hungary, India, Israel, Japan, Pakistan, Poland, Rumania, Czechoslovakia, and the Soviet Union. All of the work is devoted to nonmilitary research. It is conceivable that the basic idea of CERN could be expanded to include regional world institutes in the natural sciences, to which might be added the social sciences and the humanities, with students drawn from all parts of the world. Participants in the CERN project testify to the great value of the international aspect of work in the laboratories and the scientific community gathered together in Geneva.

European Centre for the Co-ordination of Research and Documentation in the Social Sciences, Bauernmarkt 6, Vienna 1, Austria. In pursuance of the resolution adopted by the General Conference of UNESCO at its Twelfth Session, the European Centre for the Co-ordination of Research and Documentation in the Social Sciences was organized in Vienna, following a decision taken by the Executive Committee of the International Social Science Council (ISSC) during its meeting in that city on April 5–6, 1963. The purpose of the Centre is to stimulate comparative research in the priority areas selected by its directing bodies, to coordinate such research, and to encourage the building up of appropriate documentation for the selected areas.

The Centre is a permanent external body of the International Social Science Council and has a Steering Committee whose members are appointed by the Executive Committee of the ISSC.

The first Steering Committee, appointed for two years (subsequent nominations will be for three years) was composed of the following individuals: Chairman, Professor A. Schaff (Poland); Vice-Chairman, Professor E. A. G. Robinson, (United Kingdom); Committee members, Professor A. A. Arzumanian (USSR), Professor S. Groenman (Netherlands), Rector L. Kerschagel (Austria), Professor A. Knapp (Czechoslovakia), Professor J. Stoetzel (France). The Directorate includes a scientific director acting provisionally as director of the Centre, and an administrative secretary acting provisionally as general secretary.

The actual work of the Centre began on November 1, 1963, and, for the present, its research program is concentrated on seven main fields: comparative studies of programming and planning, social consequences of industrialization, social and legal aspects of industrialization, the problem of under-developed areas in economically developed countries, time budgets, comparison of concepts and methods of aiding developing countries, and peace research.

Were it possible to expand the research topics and a curriculum into the humanities and the natural sciences, the Vienna Centre would become a full-bodied world university. The model is an appropriate one for other research and educational institutes and for regional world centers, since it includes scholars from the major cultural and geographical areas of the world, with the present exception of Communist China.

International Atomic Energy Agency (IAEA), Kaerntnerring, Vienna I, Austria. The statute for the IAEA was approved on October 26, 1956, at a conference held at the United Nations headquarters in New York and came into effect on July 29, 1957, when the United States ratified the treaty. The Agency, while not a specialized organ of the UN, is under UN auspices. In the field of atomic energy, the Agency represents one sector of need for a world research and planning body and, as such, has great educational possibilities for the future. The Agency is concerned with: 1] fundamental techniques in the field of nuclear energy; 2] theoretical and experimental aspects of the science and technology of nuclear energy; and 3] advanced training, including active participation in research work, for persons potentially qualified to carry out research programs in the basic sciences and engineering.

The Agency is supported by pledges from member states. The countries which presently belong to the IAEA are: Argentina, Australia, Austria, Brazil, Canada, Ceylon, Republic of China, Denmark, Finland, France, Germany, Greece, India, Iraq, Israel, Italy, Japan, Korea, Mexico, Monaco, Netherlands, Norway, Pakistan, Philippines, Poland, Portugal, Republic of South Africa, Switzerland, Sweden, Thailand, United Arab Republic, United Kingdom, United States, Venezuela, and Yugoslavia. Fellowships are awarded to nationals of member states who then go for training in countries with well-developed programs in atomic energy. It offers training at both undergraduate and graduate levels, with the more qualified applicants being sent for doctoral studies.

In October, 1964, the IAEA created the International Center for Theoretical Physics, located in Trieste, as a contribution to international collaboration in science and to physics in developing countries. During the first year of operation the staff of fifty-two consisted of twenty-eight nationalities, the majority coming from Latin America, East Europe, Africa, and Asia. The center is established for a period of four years with its continued existence dependent on the decisions of the atomic energy commissions of the IAEA's member states.

International Children's Centre, Chateau de Longchamp, Bois de Boulogne, Paris 16, France, is the joint effort of intergovernmental arrangements and agreements. It also cooperates closely with UNICEF and WHO. The Centre is open to nationals of all countries, and it offers training courses in maternity and child welfare, social pediatrics, child behavior and development, nutrition, and all fields related to child welfare. Depending on the particular field of study, courses run from six weeks to one year or longer. These courses are usually at a graduate or postgraduate level, and trainees are generally those whose professions are directly related to the field of child welfare.

In most cases the students are awarded scholarships by the Centre; these scholarships cover tuition, travel expenses during the course, and spending money. The cost of transportation for the participant to travel to and from the Centre is usually provided by the cooperating government or, in rare cases, by the participant himself. A student who is involved in a six-month course is awarded a scholarship amounting to $2000, while a one-year course entitles the student to a scholarship amounting to not less than $3000.

International Computation Centre, Palazzo degli Offici, Zona dell' EUR, Rome, Italy is an intergovernmental agency and its principal concern is with providing training in the processing of information and in applied mathematics. As of 1964, the member countries of the International Computation Centre are: Argentina, Belgium, Ceylon, Cuba, France, Israel, Italy, Japan, Libya, Mexico, and the United Arab Republic. Courses range from six to twelve months, and the Centre awards scholarships to the trainees.

International Conferences on Science and World Affairs (Pugwash—COSWA), 8 Asmara Road, London N.W.2, England. The Pugwash Conferences were first suggested by Lord Bertrand Russell in an appeal he made from London on July 10, 1955. Other cosponsors and cosigners of the written appeal included Albert Einstein, Frederic Joliot-Curie, Hideki Yukawa, and other eminent scientists from Great Britain and the United States. The Russell statement follows.

140

In the tragic situation that confronts humanity, we feel that scientists should assemble in conferences to appraise the perils that have arisen as a result of the development of weapons of mass destruction. . . . We are speaking on this occasion, not as members of this or that nation, continent or creed, but as human beings, members of the species man, whose continued existence is in doubt. The world is full of conflicts; and, overshadowing all minor conflicts, the titanic struggle between communism and anti-communism.

Most of us are not neutral in feeling but, as human beings, we have to remember that if the issues between East and West are to be decided in any manner that can give satisfaction to anybody, whether Communist or anti-Communist, whether Asian or European or American, whether white or black, then these issues must not be decided by war. We should wish this to be understood, both in the East and the West.

We invite this congress to be convened, and through it the scientists of the world and the general public should subscribe to the following resolution:

"In view of the fact that in any future war nuclear weapons will certainly be employed, and that such weapons threaten the continued existence of mankind, we urge the governments of the world to realize, and to acknowledge publicly, that their purposes cannot be furthered by a world war, and we urge them, consequently, to find peaceful means for the settlement of all matters of dispute between them."

Though the appeal was made in 1955, there was no perceptible movement in the direction suggested by its initiators until Lord Russell gained the interest of American industrialist, Cyrus Eaton. With Mr. Eaton's financial backing, a group of scientists from East and West met at his summer home in Pugwash, Nova Scotia, for the first of what later proved to be a series of conferences of scientists from the two major ideological blocs. This conference, which took place July 6–11, 1957, was attended by scientists from the United States (seven), the

USSR (three), Australia, Canada, Great Britain, France, Nationalist China, and Poland. The second conference, which took place in Lac Beauport, Quebec, from March 31 to April 11, 1958, had the active participation of scientists from the United States, the USSR, Canada, Australia, Great Britain, West Germany, and Communist China. Although invited each year, Communist Chinese scientists have not attended during the past five years. Beginning in 1958, there have been two COSWA conferences every year.

COSWA has been officially endorsed by the Soviet Academy of Sciences, the American Academy of Arts and Sciences, and comparable organizations in the participating countries. By 1962, when the ninth and tenth Pugwash Conferences were held, participation—both in terms of individuals attending and countries represented—increased markedly. The ninth conference, which took place in Cambridge, England, was attended by sixty scientists from eighteen countries; the tenth, in London, brought together two hundred scientists from thirty-six countries, including an eighteen-member Soviet delegation and some top experts and government advisors from the United States and Great Britain.

To add permanence to the conferences, a Continuing Committee was set up at the third conference in Kitzbuehel, Austria. The composition of the Committee shows a degree of cooperation between East and West; it consists, at present, of three Soviet scientists, three Americans, three British, and one scientist each from Italy, France, Poland, and India. The efforts of COSWA members to achieve a solution to the problem of atomic bomb testing are considered to have had an important part in bringing about the test-ban treaty in 1963. Were it possible to develop a year-round program of research, study, and education in science and society through COSWA at a central place, the world university idea would be achieved in considerable measure.

International Schools Association and *International Schools Examination Syndicate*, 62 route de Chene, Geneva, Switzerland.

In collaboration with the International School of Geneva, the International Schools Association has developed a pilot project in international examinations for the graduates of secondary schools, with the intention of providing international standards of entrance to universities throughout the world. Such an international system, if carried out on a large scale, will have great significance in the creation of new forms of world education in the universities.

Should it prove possible to establish a network of universities which recognize the international examination, and to link it with a network of the world's secondary schools which agree to develop curricula adapted to the standards of the examination, it will be possible for students educated in one national educational system to move easily to the universities of other countries. The circulation of the world's students would then become infinitely more possible and potentially more desirable.

Already progress has been made in this direction with the development of an examination in Contemporary History 1913–1963, administered for the first time in June, 1963, at the International School in Geneva. Subsequently, the syllabus and examination papers were sent to all ministries of education and departments of education throughout the world, with some forty favorable responses. With the cooperation of UNESCO, curricula and examinations are being developed in all areas. An international board is in the process of formation to supervise further work and to continue the analysis of existing syllabi of national educational systems, to select what is appropriate, and to broaden the conception of the various disciplines, categories, and teaching methods into world dimensions.

International Secretariat for Volunteer Service (*ISVS*), Washington, D. C. 20525 was created by forty-one governments attending the International Conference on Human Skills in the Decade of Development (Middle Level Manpower Conference) in Puerto Rico, October 10–12, 1962. Its purpose is to support and assist national volunteer service programs by serving as an information exchange and clearinghouse, by encouraging more

143

programs of this kind and helping to set up and operate them, and by cooperating with other interested organizations with a view to increasing "the supply and quality of middle level manpower available to developing countries."

The Secretariat is financed by voluntary contributions of member countries and staffed by an international group from Germany, Israel, the Netherlands, and the Philippines. Seven regional meetings have been held in the past two years for discussion of common problems, and meetings were held in Africa, Latin America, and the Far East in the latter part of 1965. Teams of international experts are sent to interested countries on request. Should the Secretariat develop an educational program to prepare youth for voluntary service "while at the same time promoting better understanding between people of different cultures," a genuine world college might emerge from the present organization.

United Nations International School (*UNIS*), First Ave. and 70th St., New York, N. Y., was established in 1947, in Lake Success, New York, to meet the needs of members of the UN Secretariat and Delegations for the education of their children. From the start, the philosophy of the School called for the preservation of the cultural values of each nationality while practicing the ideals of international understanding and cooperation of the UN Charter. An association of parents and friends of the School began nursery-school classes in 1947, in the guest house of the then UN headquarters in Lake Success with twenty children from fifteen countries and a faculty of four teachers, each of a different nationality. By September, 1949, the first elementary class had been started, with a higher grade added each year until the ultimate objective was realized in 1961–62 of six years of elementary, four of secondary and three of preuniversity education. When the UN moved to its present headquarters in 1950, the School moved into a group of converted apartments in Parkway Village, Jamaica, New York. In 1959, temporary quarters were obtained in Public School 82 in

Manhattan to house all thirteen grades. These premises and the Parkway Village feeder school through the fifth grade will be maintained until September, 1968.

During the academic year 1964–65, the School had 568 pupils from sixty-eight countries, including 30 from the Eastern European Socialist Republics, 3 from Cuba and 14 from the USSR. Of these 568 pupils, 310 were children of those working in the UN Secretariat, 50 were children of UN Delegation members, 55 were of international origin not connected with the UN, and 175 were Americans. Children of local U. S. citizens made up approximately 30 per cent of the enrollment. There were forty-six full-time and three part-time members on the academic staff, nine from Asia, one from the Middle East and one from Africa, one from South America, seven from North America, twenty-eight from Europe, and two from Australia.

The objectives of the School curriculum are to "provide a unique opportunity for the development of international and inter-cultural understanding. . . . This, however, does not mean that the School is a denationalizing institution. On the contrary, its aim is to maintain each student's pride in and knowledge of his own culture. It aims also at providing for a mastery of the basic skills of communication and calculation, as far as feasible, in the home language of the pupil as well as in the language of his or her environment. . . . The School tries to ensure that the child develops in harmony with his age group requirements, in harmony with his environment, and in harmony both with his national culture and the wider world community." Policy for the conduct of the UNIS is set by an eighteen-member Board of Trustees; administration of the School, its management and its operation are the tasks of the Director, appointed by the Board. In addition to managing the day-to-day affairs of the School, the Director is responsible for the establishment of educational methods, curricula, and standards; the administration of the budget, and the making of all appointments. Apart from establishing policy for the conduct of

145

the School, the Board of Trustees is also concerned with its development and with raising funds for the School's advancement.

The importance of the School to the United Nations is recognized in the financial support given to it by the UN General Assembly which has made grants-in-aid since 1949, ranging from $7,400 in 1952 to $100,000 in 1959 and later years. On February 10, 1965, the UN General Assembly passed a resolution which approved plans for the construction of a $7,000,000 building and campus with facilities for one thousand children. The new building at Twenty-fifth Street and Franklin D. Roosevelt Drive, to be completed by September, 1968, is made possible by a gift of up to $7,500,000 from the Ford Foundation, conditional on the School becoming self-supporting. A three million dollar fund-raising drive is now under way to ensure that the School can become independent of additional UN contributions.

The United Nations International School is one of the first of its kind in the world, and can serve as an example for the development of similar schools and world colleges on a regional basis on other continents. It can also serve as an experimental center for the development of world curricula and for the creation of an international baccalaureate degree.

United Nations Institute for Training and Research, 801 United Nations Plaza, New York, New York. Resolution 1827 (xvii) of the General Assembly proposed the creation of the United Nations Institute for Training and Research (UNITAR). During the next session, resolution 1934 authorized the Secretary-General to take necessary steps to establish the Institute and to explore possible governmental and nongovernmental sources of financial assistance. In its broadest terms the purpose of the Institute is to enhance the effectiveness of the United Nations in pursuing its two overriding objectives—the maintenance of peace and security and the promotion of economic and social development. The Institute will provide facilities for certain

146

types of training and research which are of high priority in advancing toward these objectives.

By March, 1965, the Secretary-General had appointed and convened UNITAR's Board of Trustees, which is now composed of seventeen distinguished members of international reputation in fields of interest to the United Nations, drawn from different regions of the world and representing different political and cultural backgrounds, two United Nations Undersecretaries and four *ex-officio* members: the Secretary-General, the President of the General Assembly, the President of the Economic and Social Council, and the Executive Director of the Institute. Mr. Kenneth Younger of Great Britain, director of the Royal Institute of International Affairs, is the elected Board Chairman; the countries represented on the Board are Belgium, Canada, Chile, Denmark, France, India, Iran, Kenya, United Arab Republic, United Kingdom, United States, and Venezuela.

After consultation with the Board of Trustees, the Secretary-General announced in March, 1965 the appointment of Gabriel d'Arboussier of Senegal as Executive Director of the Institute, with the terms and conditions of service of a UN Undersecretary. The Board of Trustees is responsible for determining the basic policies of the Institute and for adopting its budget on the basis of the proposals submitted by the Executive Director, who has an overall responsibility for the organization, direction, and administration of the Institute, in accordance with the general policies formulated by the Board of Trustees.

The Institute's envisioned budget for the first five to six years is $10,000,000. As of November, 1965, sixty-five countries in Asia, Africa, and South America had pledged or paid total contributions of $5,723,355.

In the field of training an agreement was reached on the transfer to the Institute of certain existing training programs within the UN Secretariat. These are: the Training Program for Foreign Service Officers from Newly Developing Countries, the Training Program in Development Financing, and the Training Program in Techniques and Procedures of Technical

Assistance. A projected program for the training of assistant resident representatives and counterpart personnel, which has been accepted in principle, is under preparation.

The Executive Director submitted to the Board at its third session, in March, 1966, criteria and standards to govern the general and special fellowships which are to be established, including the UNITAR Adlai Stevenson Fellowships.

A few preliminary studies are now being carried out in connection with research. The Executive Director has agreed, in principle, with the Director of the World Food Program, that the Institute might undertake an evaluation of some of the Program's activities, and technical discussions are now being held on the application of this agreement. Execution of this research project, in addition to being of special interest to the World Food Program, will take the Institute into the general field of evaluation, in which, by means of comparative studies, an attempt will be made gradually to develop a methodology. Preliminary studies are being carried out on two other subjects with a particular effort to avoid duplication. These are: language teaching and a directory of existing training and research institutes.

Further research possibilities have been discussed and recommended by the Board of Trustees. These include a survey of existing studies on the instrumentalities of UN peace-keeping, a feasibility study on technological and scientific resources released by disarmament for purposes of economic and social development, and a study of UN methods and techniques for the promotion and protection of human rights. The training and research activities of the Institute will be closely interrelated. It is intended that the training program will benefit from the analysis and evaluations performed in the field of research, and that, in turn, it should be possible for the Institute's research work to profit from the highly qualified personnel participating in the training programs. The value of the group which would be associated with the Institute in both fields need not be limited to the accomplishment of their immediate tasks. Their studies

148

and contacts with the UN may also build a relationship of great potential value.

The Institute's headquarters are located in its own building, opposite the headquarters of the United Nations Secretariat itself, since the range of the Institute's interests will be so closely related to the activities of the United Nations. The Rockefeller Foundation contributed $450,000 for a building to house the Institute. Much of its operation, however, will be decentralized; aside from its Geneva office, the Institute may administer various research and training activities in other locations, as appropriate.

The second category includes organizations and institutions based on international concepts although operating regionally.

Albert Schweitzer College, Corcelles sur Chavornay, Switzerland, was founded in Churwalden, Switzerland, in 1950. The College offers the equivalent of a junior year course of study in the liberal arts with emphasis on tutorial instruction. The student body, faculty, and board represent many nationalities, and instruction is trilingual. The purpose of the College is described as a "one world college dedicated to the ideals of scholarship, religious freedom, international understanding, personal service, and reverence for life that were so eminently characteristic of the great man for whom it is named. Living and working together in an intimate community, young men and women study under the close personal and scholarly guidance of a faculty devoted to Dr. Schweitzer's ideal of service."

Atlantic College in the United Kingdom, St. Donat's Castle, Glamorgan, South Wales. College in this case can be misleading, because of the interchangeability of this term when used by the English. This College aims to promote and provide international education at preuniversity but post-high school level, i.e., at the British sixth form level. According to the *Half-Yearly*

149

Progress Report (October, 1964), the aims of the College are:

> To promote international understanding through education; to break down national barriers in education particularly in the field of university admission, and to make education a force which unites, not divides. To achieve this, we intend to establish not just one College, but a number of Sixth Form colleges, each of which will offer to selected boys of different nationalities and high ability a two-year academic course immediately before entering universities in their own or other countries.
>
> To provide education specifically designed to meet future needs, to give first-hand knowledge of the outlook of other nations, and to stress the teaching of foreign languages.
>
> To promote physical fitness and to satisfy the youthful instinct for adventure; to foster a spirit of compassion and a sense of obligation to the community.

In 1964, the College had 156 students from twenty-one countries (Argentina, Bermuda, Brazil, Burma, Canada, Denmark, France, Germany, Greece, Iran, Italy, Jordan, Lebanon, Malawi, Malta, Mexico, the Netherlands, Norway, Sweden, the United Kingdom, and the United States). The biggest proportion, sixty-eight students, were from the United Kingdom; part of the student body had financial assistance in the form of scholarships. Financial support took the form of grants from the British Government and business concerns.

The Center for Cultural and Technical Interchange Between East and West (The East-West Center) was established in October, 1960, by the United States Congress, by a rider to the Mutual Security Act of that year authorizing the State Department to provide a grant in aid to the University of Hawaii for the Center's establishment. It is administered by a Chancellor, responsible to the President of the University of Hawaii and the University's Board of Regents. Its budget is determined by the House Subcommittee on Appropriations for the State Department and administered by the Board of Regents of the University of Hawaii. Approximately $37,000,000 for buildings and operation of the program have so far been assigned.

The Center consists of three main divisions: 1] the Institute for Technical Interchange, which trains students principally for the U. S. Agency for International Development;   2] the Institute for Advanced Projects, the research arm of the Center; and   3] the Institute for Student Interchange. The purpose of the East West Center is stated as "the promotion of mutual understanding among the countries of Asia and the Pacific and the U. S." In pursuit of this aim, scholars and intellectuals from the U. S. and Asian countries come to the Center for a year's residence, and for attendance at four- to six-week seminars and week-long conferences. Research, articles and books on Asian development and Asian-American relations are developed. Students at the center come from twenty-seven Asian-Pacific countries and from the United States, the ratio being approximately three Americans to one Asian.

The potential, in this instance, of developing a genuine world center for the study of cultural, social, political, and economic problems, awaits only a shift in thinking on the part of the State Department and the administrative officers of the University away from the bilateral cultural arrangements now made between Eastern countries and the United States, and a move toward a broader conception of the role of the U. S. in bringing about world understanding through education.

College of Europe, Dyver 11, Bruges, Belgium, was established at the European Cultural Conference in Lausanne in December, 1949, after a three-week preparatory session held in Bruges. The first academic year began in the fall of 1950. As part of the trend toward European integration, the College was to be a graduate research center to study the political, economic, social, and cultural problems presented by the union of Europe.

The curriculum was not narrowly conceived to train civil servants for emerging European institutions but as a broadening of the mind and the development of a common point of view through an international and interdisciplinary approach. The course of study is eight months, and the College has sought to enable the students to become more completely aware of European realities through a general understanding of at least one other field of knowledge in addition to that in which he had previously studied. However, with the development of new European institutions, such as the Common Market, the European Coal and Steel Community, the instruction has assumed a more technical character to provide specialists to give leadership to these new institutions.

Six of the faculty are permanent staff, and visiting professors of different nationalities come at regular intervals. Eighty-five per cent of the student body of approximately fifty are from Western Europe with some students from Eastern Europe—from twelve to eighteen nationalities are represented. All students and resident faculty live in a large hotel with community life considered an essential element of the College.

Half of the finances of the College of Europe are provided by the Belgian government; the remainder by the Federal Republic of Germany, Great Britain, Luxembourg, the Netherlands, France, the European Coal and Steel Community, and the town of Bruges. Other governments or institutions subsidize the College through scholarships. However, the College of Europe is independent of any government or intergovernmental organization.

Common Market European Schools, Conseil Supérieur de l'Ecole Européene, Boulevarde de la Foire, Luxembourg. A system of secondary schools has been developed in the last ten years to serve primarily the needs of the children of the officials of the coal and steel organization of the European Common Market. The first school was organized at Luxembourg, in 1956, and other schools have been established in Brussels, Varese (near Milano), Karlsruhe, Mol (near Antwerp), and Putten (near Amsterdam). The schools are financed by the

respective ministries of education of the six governments participating in the Common Market and by the coal and steel community organizations.

The ministries of education of the six governments appoint
an overall governing board which plans the curriculum; each of
the schools is administered locally by a board chosen by the
higher body and local parent and teacher organizations.

The faculties represent the six nationalities of the Common
Market and are appointed by the respective ministries. The
headmaster of each school is appointed for a five-year term only,
after which he is to be replaced by someone of another nationality.

The curriculum prepares students for a European baccalaureate which is designed to meet the university entrance requirements of all six Common Market nations, i.e., the French
Baccalauréat, the German Arbitur, and university entrance requirements in the Netherlands, Belgium, Luxembourg, and Italy.
The instruction is in Flemish, Italian, German, and French with
English as a compulsory third language. All students are bilingual and many are trilingual.

European Institute for Advanced International Studies, Nice,
France, was founded in 1965, by the International Center for
European Training (C.I.F.E.) under the leadership of M. Alex-
andre Marc with the intention that it would be the beginning of
an international university. This international university is to be
composed of a consortium of graduate institutes, each dealing
with some aspect of international and human relations and each
founded and administered by one or more universities from
countries in the Atlantic community, such as the United States,
Great Britain, France, Germany, and Italy. The project received the support of the city of Nice which provided land, the
beginning operating budget, and administrative buildings.
Classrooms and other teaching facilities are provided by the
University of Nice.

The first semester of the European Institute began in April,

1965, with thirty-one students from Europe, North and South America, and Africa and thirty professors from Europe and North America. The teaching and research at the Institute are centered around an interdisciplinary study of federalism, both in theory and as applied to European integration, Atlantic relations, and the developing countries. Additional institutes to be established at the Nice center will be Atlantic studies, East-West studies, study of the developing areas, study of American federalism, Latin American studies, and ethnopsychology. The international university is dedicated to the creation of new European and Atlantic scholars, capable of meeting the international issues of the modern world, while at the same time serving as a link among the countries of the Atlantic community.

Friends World Institute, 5722 Northern Boulevard, East Norwich, New York. After five years of work by the Committee on a Friends World College, a New York State group of the Society of Friends (Quakers), the Friends World Institute opened in September, 1965, with thirty-eight students and nine faculty. The Institute will become Friends World College as soon as its assets and campus qualify it for a New York charter. The Institute is temporarily located at Mitchell Gardens, Westbury, New York, and is actively seeking a permanent campus in the area.

The Institute is an experiment in international and polycultural higher education based on a study of world problems. The four-year program involves six-month stays at each of seven centers around the world. For the first six-month period, the students attended seminars on various social problems and made an extended trip to Washington, through Appalachia and the deep South, observing and discussing poverty, regional development, the T.V.A., civil rights, cooperatives, and Indian affairs. Then the class moved to Mexico for five months and will go to Scandinavia for study of Western Europe.

The Institute is initially organized into four programs: The Division for Resident Study maintains a campus in the United

154

States with a resident four-year program leading to the B.A. degree. The Division of Study Centers Abroad will operate through seven strategically selected centers where a student will gain knowledge of the world through living, travelling, studying, and working for six months in each region. The Center for Peace Studies and Research will provide a graduate program leading to the M.A. degree, and The Summer Study-Travel Program will operate a series of trips abroad for students in the Division of Resident Study.

Graduate Institute of International Studies, 132 rue de Lausanne, Geneva, Switzerland, was established in 1927 "to maintain . . . a center for the study of contemporary international questions from the judicial, political, and economic points of view." Associated with the University of Geneva, the Graduate Institute has approximately one hundred and fifty students who are mostly doctoral candidates from America and Europe and a faculty which is predominantly European. The curriculum in the social sciences is taught from an international perspective through lectures, seminars, and student research.

Middle East Technical University (METU), 24 Mudafaa Caddesi, Yenisehir, Ankara, Turkey, provides an illuminating example of possibilities for future developments of the world university idea. The idea for METU originated in 1954, during a visit by Mr. Charles Abrams of the United States on behalf of the United Nations. Mr. Abrams originally suggested a School of Architecture and City Planning for Turkey; following the work of a UN Technical Assistance Mission in Turkey in 1955, the idea was expanded to include engineering and technological disciplines. With the help of UNESCO, a group of Turkish business, industrial, and educational leaders drew up a university charter which was approved by the Grand National Assembly of Turkey in 1959. In the beginning, only courses in architecture were available, but faculties in Engineering, the Arts and Sciences, and the Administrative Sciences were added,

155

and the University expanded its concept in an international direction to serve the needs of the Middle East region rather than simply those of Turkey. "It is of incalculable value," says the METU catalog, "in building understanding between nations for students of different origins and backgrounds to work and mingle together." There are faculty members from twenty countries, an international student body of three thousand with plans for an eventual enrollment of twelve thousand.

In the beginning, METU received financial help from the UN Expanded Program of Technical Assistance, and now receives funds from the United States AID program, the Ford Foundation, CENTO, and from "friendly foreign governments in the way of experts, equipment and books under bilateral agreements." The main source of funds is, however, the budget of the Turkish Ministry of Education. It is significant that the conception of a technical university should have expanded in the direction of including the arts and sciences, education and public administration, thus uniting technical and liberal studies through the demands of the region which METU serves. It is entirely possible that through expansion of the basic idea of a regional center for technical and social planning into that of a world center serving regional and world needs in the arts and sciences as well as in the technologies, the evolution of METU into a world university could take place.

New Experimental College, Slotsherrensvej 21, Vanløse, Copenhagen, Denmark was established in 1962 by Aage R. Nielsen as an "educational community designed to give students and professors from all countries an opportunity to study, do research, and work together to develop a world university." The curriculum is determined by students and faculty on the basis of interest and has concentrated mainly on philosophy, economics, and the nature of democracy. The faculty teach without salary in order to be involved in a training laboratory for their own personal development. Since 1962 approximately two hundred persons have been involved in the College, about half of whom are regular students. The College is financed largely by student fees, and facilities in Copenhagen provide for thirty students with a center in Thy being developed for one hundred students.

Patrice Lumumba University of Friendship Among Nations (Patrice Lumumba University or Friendship University), 5 Donskoy Proyesd, 7, Moscow, U.S.S.R., was founded in 1960, by the government of the U.S.S.R. and was named after the Congolese political leader. Admission is open mainly to students from Asian, African, and Latin-American countries.

The University offers courses in engineering, agriculture, medicine, physico-mathematical sciences, natural sciences, history and philology, economics, national economic planning, and international law.

Most, if not all, of the students attending the university are holders of scholarships provided by the Soviet government. These scholarships cover tuition, free medical care, transportation to and from Moscow, a monthly allowance of ninety rubles for undergraduates and one hundred rubles for graduate students, and an allowance of three hundred rubles for the purchase of warm clothing. Each student pays his own board. In addition, students spending their summer and winter holidays in the Soviet Union are taken on "guided tours" at no cost.

Courses at the undergraduate level take five to six years; while graduate courses may extend from three to four years, including a one-year course in the Russian language. By 1964, there were 2,100 students enrolled at the University, with more than eighty countries represented. The University graduated its first class (228) on June 29, 1965. The entire cost of running the University is borne by the Soviet government. Administration rests with the Rector, the Pro-Rectors, and the Academic Council, which together constitute the University Senate.

Visva Bharati, Santineketan, District of Birbhum, West Bengal, India, was founded by Rabindranath Tagore in 1921, ninety-three miles from Calcutta, as a world center for the study of international culture and the promotion of interracial amity and intercultural understanding. Courses included studies in painting, music, oriental languages, philosophy, and literature. In 1951, by an Act of the Indian Parliament, Visva Bharati was incorporated as a residential university for study and teaching, as part of the system of Indian universities. The student body and faculty are international, the curriculum has an intercultural, international character, although the bulk of the students and teachers are Indian and Asian.

World University—International Institute of the Americas, P.O. Box 22876, University Station, San Juan, Puerto Rico, opened in the fall of 1965, as the first unit of World University. The founding of this Western Hemisphere institute is to be followed by the establishment of similar institutes in Africa, Asia, and other continents of the world. Each institute will feature the history, culture, and civilization of that continent in relation to the rest of the world. Dr. Ronald Bauer, Chancellor of the Institute, has stated that "education must be made available for all people on this earth, and it must be education with an international perspective. This World University system through its interrelated institutes on each continent will seek to break through the artificial barriers of history, custom and traditions, habits and politics, and antagonisms based on race, religion, nationalism, ignorance, poverty, greed or any other condition that tends to lower the dignity and well being of man anywhere." The International Institute of the Americas will stress the culture of Latin America and the United States, emphasizing the cultural contributions, common history, and problems of the Americas.

Another aim of the International Institute of the Americas is to offer a fully interrelated system of education that provides a formal educational program throughout life, beginning with the nursery school and continuing through elementary and secondary school, university, graduate, and adult studies with a special college for retired people who wish to continue their education.

The Center for Undergraduate Studies, the Graduate Center for Inter-American Studies, the College for Adults, and the College of the Emeriti are the first to be organized with four hundred students attending the opening session of the Center for Undergraduate Studies and one hundred attending the centers for adult education. The faculty of fifteen are drawn from the Western Hemisphere and Europe, and an International Advisory Council includes Don Pablo Casals and Madame Pandit.

B A selection of organizations and associations interested in the concept of world education

A COMPREHENSIVE LIST of such organizations may be found in *The World of Learning 1965–66*, 16th ed. London, Europa Publications Ltd., 1966.

Center for Human Understanding
  2726 N St., Washington, D. C.
Education and World Affairs
  522 Fifth Ave., New York, New York
Friends World Committee for Consultation
  Woodbrooke, Selly Oak, Birmingham 29, England
  AMERICAN SECTION:
  152-A North 15th St., Philadelphia, Pennsylvania
Hague Academy of International Law
  Peace Palace, The Hague, Netherlands

Institute for International Order
11 West 42nd St., New York, New York
International Association for the Advancement of Educational Research
Schlossstrasse 29, Frankfurt/M.W., Germany
International Association for the Exchange of Students for Technical Experience
Kennedy Allee 50, 532 Bad Godesberg, Germany
International Association of Universities
% International Universities Bureau
6 rue Franklin, Paris 16, France
International Association of University Professors and Lecturers
Rozier 6, Ghent, Belgium
International Council for Philosophy and Humanistic Studies
UNESCO House, 6 rue Franklin, Paris 16, France
International Council of Scientific Unions
2 Via Sebenico, Rome, Italy
International Economic Association
92 rue d'Assas, Paris, France
International Institute for Educational Planning
7 rue Eugene Delacroix, Paris 16, France
International Institute for Labor Studies
154 route de Lausanne, Geneva, Switzerland
U.S.A. OFFICE: 917 Fifteenth St., N.W., Washington, D. C.
International Peace Research Association
Polemological Institute, Ubbo, Emminsingel 19, Groningen, Netherlands
International Political Science Association
27 rue Saint-Guillaume, Paris 7, France
International Social Science Council
UNESCO House-Annex, 6 rue Franklin, Paris 16, France
International Sociological Association
Case Postale 141, Les Acacias, Geneva, Switzerland
International Theatre Institute
UNESCO House-Annex, 6 rue Franklin, Paris 16, France
International University of Comparative Sciences
13 rue du Post, Luxembourg, Belgium

New Education Fellowship
   55 Upper Stone St., Tunbridge Wells, Kent, England
Society for the Psychological Study of Social Issues
   P.O. Box 1248, Ann Arbor, Michigan
United Nations Educational, Scientific and Cultural Organization
   Place de Fontenoy, Paris 7, France
UNESCO Institute for Education
   Feldbrunnenstrasse 70, Hamburg 13, West Germany
UN Research Institute for Social Development
   1 Ave. de la Paix, Geneva, Switzerland
World Academy of Art and Science
   1 Ruppin St., Rehovot, Israel
World Association of World Federalists
   Burgemeester Patijhlaah 49, The Hague, Netherlands
World Confederation of Organizations of the Teaching Profession
   1330 Massachusetts Ave., N.W., Washington, D. C.
World Federation of United Nations Associations
   1 Ave. de la Paix, Geneva, Switzerland
   U.S.A. OFFICE: *Room 1055, United Nations Building, New York, New York*
World Organization for Early Childhood Education
   134 bd. Berthier, Paris 17, France
World University Service
   13 rue Calvin, Geneva, Switzerland
World Veterans Federation
   16 rue Hamelin, Paris 16, France

c Some proposals for a world

university

THE FOLLOWING is a sampling of the proposals made by individuals and organizations for establishing a world university or an international institution of higher learning which is fully internationalized. The list is by no means complete, but it is representative.

African Students Foundation of Canada. Proposal to the Canadian Government to establish a United Nations University at Uranium City, Elliot Lake, Ontario. Address: J. S. Grant, Seaton Development Ltd., 6 Tippet Road, Downsview, Ontario, Canada.

Association for Commitment to World Responsibility, University of Michigan student-faculty organization. The following documents are available: *A United Nations University* (third draft copy) 1962. "A College of International Administration" (unpublished) and "A United Nations University Service Corps" (unpublished) 1962, by Stephen A. Fraser. "Comments and Elaborations on the Objectives and Functions of a United Nations University" (unpublished) and "The Concept of an International University" (unpublished) 1962, by Elton B. McNeil. Address: Student Activities Building, University of Michigan, Ann Arbor, Michigan.

Avery, J. H. Brochure, *The Why, What and How of the World University* (Boyd Printing Co., Panama City, Florida, 1956).

Barany, R., M.D., Sweden. Proposal to the Committee on Intellectual Cooperation, League of Nations, 1925, for establishing an "International University for the Training of Statesmen, Diplomats, Politicians, Political Editors and Professors in High Schools of Political Science."

Bedrosian, Max, and Paul Obler, American educators. Proposal to UNESCO for establishing a series of United Nations University Centers around the world, to be administered by UNESCO and financed by the United Nations. "United Nations University Centers: A Proposal to Extend International Understanding Through Education" (unpublished) April, 1959. Address: Newark State College, Newark, New Jersey.

Berne, Henry, Associate Director, Airlie Foundation. Proposal for a polycultural institution from primary through graduate level called "The Bridge" with a college focusing on teacher education and a secondary school to be the first established. Address: Warrenton, Virginia.

Canadian Home and School and Parent-Teacher Federation of Canada, World University Committee; Chairman, C. M. Bedford. Presentation to the Minister of External Affairs advocating a feasibility study of a proposal for a world university to be established by the Canadian Government. Mimeographed. Address: 370 Dundas Street, West, Toronto 2B, Ontario, Canada.

164

Center for Human Understanding; Chairman, John Nef. Preliminary proposal for establishing a world university through joint planning by interested scholars in various countries. Address: 2726 N Street, N.W., Washington, D.C. 20007.

Committee for the Promotion of an International University in America; Secretary, Professor George Geng. A Committee assembled by the late William Heard Kilpatrick proposed an international university to be established in America with a full international curriculum, student body and faculty. "An International University in America" (unpublished) 1961. Address: Glassboro State Teachers College, Glassboro, New Jersey.

Committee on a Friends World College. "A Proposal for a Friends World College" (unpublished) 1960. "Progress Report" (unpublished) July, 1961. "Summer Project" (unpublished) 1963. Address: 5722 Northern Boulevard, East Norwich, New York.

Federation for a United Nations University; Chairman, Dr. George Huthsteiner. Address: 23055 Ostronic Drive, Woodland Hills, California.

Federation of American Scientists Committee for a United Nations University; Chairman, Professor Evan Kane. "Proposal to Study the Founding of a United Nations University" (unpublished) July, 1958. Address: Federation of American Scientists, 2025 Eye Street, Washington, D. C.

Gomez, Julian. "A World University" (unpublished). Address: 430 West 125th Street, New York, New York.

Hefter, Edward J. Report to Edward J. Hefter Foundation, April, 1964. Address: 5555 Northwest Highway, Chicago 30, Illinois.

International Association of University Professors and Lecturers. Proposal for an international university, later modified to include International Institute of the Social Sciences. Described in Simey, T. S. and F. T. H. Fletcher, "Report on an International Institute of the Social Sciences," *International Social Science Bulletin of UNESCO*, III, 3 (1951).

International Society for the Establishment of a World University; Rector of experimental session, Professor E. deVries. "World University; Pioneer of Peace" (unpublished) May, 1958. Address: Seuefelderstrasse 1, Stuttgart, Germany.

Inter-National University Foundation; Chairman, Dr. Karl Ewerts. A 1962 proposal for an Inter-National University to be established on Ellis Island, New York. Address: 467 Central Park West, New York, New York 10025.

Laugier, Henri, former Assistant Secretary-General of the United Nations. Proposals for international universities and regional centers, e.g. "Pour une Université International des Pays Sous-Développés," *Bulletin of the International Association of Universities*, VIII, 3 (1960).

Marc, Alexander, British university professor. Proposal for an International University, described in "Mission of an International University," *International Social Science Bulletin of UNESCO*, IV, 1 (1952).

Swami Nityaswaru-pananda, former Secretary of Ramakrishna Mission Institute of Culture in Calcutta. *School of World Civilization*, foreword by Dr. S. Radhakrishnan, President of India (mimeographed). ". . . the integrated study of mankind's cultural and scientific development from the universal standpoint." Address: Ramakrishna Mission Institute of Culture, Calcutta, India.

Rose, Elizabeth and Luther Evans. Proposal for a two-year United Nations University to be located in Japan presented to the Japanese National Commission for UNESCO in August, 1964. Address: Mrs. Elizabeth Rose, Box 828, Route 3, Golden, Colorado.

Society for the Psychological Study of Social Issues of the American Psychological Association. "Proposal for the Establishment of a United Nations Institute of the Human Sciences" (unpublished) June, 1947. Address: American Psychological Association, 1333 Sixteenth Street, N.W., Washington, D. C.

Staley, Eugene. "A Proposal for a United Nations University" (unpublished) 1960. Address: International Industrial Development Center, Stanford Research Institute, Menlo Park, California.

Strømnes, Martin. "Creating World Universities under United Nations," (unpublished) 1962. Norwegian State College of Education, Trondheim, Norway.

Taylor, Harold, et al. "Report on the Experimental Project for a World College at Harrow Hill, Glen Head, Long Island" (unpublished) 1963. Address: 241 West 12th Street, New York, New York 10014.

Trowbridge, A. B., et al. "A Proposal to Establish a University of the United Nations" (unpublished) 1945. Address: Fairfax Road, McLean, Virginia.

Union of International Associations. Proposal by Paul Otlet for international university in Brussels. Presented to League of Nations, 1919–20. Experimental sessions were held from 1920 to 1933 when they were discontinued.

Woodroofe, Kenneth, professor of English, University of Kashmir and Jammu. "School of World Civilization, a Tentative

Suggestion for Shaping the Programme," (unpublished), prepared in relation to plan by Swami Nityaswaru-pananda.

World Academy of Art and Science; Secretary-General, Dr. Hugo Boyko. Proposal for a transnational university by establishing regional study centers in various continents. Address: P.O. Box 534, 1 Ruppin Street, Rehovot, Israel.

World Confederation of Organizations of the Teaching Profession. Proposal made to the United Nations for the establishment of an international university centered possibly in Geneva, offering a one year post-graduate course to some five hundred students, after Dwight D. Eisenhower proposed an "international school for global understanding" at the WCOTP Annual Congress in Stockholm, August, 1962. Address: 1330 Massachusetts Ave., N.W., Washington, D. C.

Yeaton, Robert Kniss. Proposal for World Center in islands of Espiritu Santo and La Partida, Mexico, "to develop a world point of view among all men . . . by bringing together the future leaders of all nations to meet with outstanding world thinkers. . . ." To be financed by a World Market located in southern portion of Epiritu Santo. Address: APDO 384, San Luis Potosi, S L P, Mexico.

Zitko, Howard John. A world university is to be established on a six-hundred acre campus near Tucson, Arizona, with regional centers elsewhere in the world. A World University Round Table was established in 1947 in California, by Dr. Zitko, Coordinator General, and has members in sixty countries. Address: P.O. Box 4800-K, University Station, Tucson, Arizona.

D   The idea of a world college*

Harold Taylor

THE IDEA of a world college has an especially persuasive power. It suggests a college unlike any now in existence, to which would come students from everywhere in the world, Communist and non-Communist, Western and Eastern, Jew and Arab, Christian and Moslem, colored and white, each of them different, each of them welcomed and cherished because of the difference. There the students would be taught, by scholars from across the world, a body of knowledge that would contain, not nationalist histories and ideologies, but the history and culture of man in the entire world. It would be a college designed to develop a new concept of the world and of education, and to act as a source of ideas and action for the achievement of world

* *Saturday Review*, November 14, 1964. By permission of the publisher.

understanding and a peaceful world order. The arts of all cultures would be practiced and studied, the ideas of all societies would have a full and fair chance to be known and valued. In a world community of the intellect, the hope of mankind for a comradely world order would be reflected, its reality anticipated.

The idea has roots in the university tradition of the West and in the cosmopolitanism of the great cities in history. There has always been an unseen international community, independent of transient governments and ideologies, among the artists, writers, scientists, and intellectuals of the world, and a mutual respect for work of quality and integrity, no matter what wars, conflicts, and antagonisms have officially existed between the governments of nation-states. It is not difficult to hope that through an increase in the traffic of ideas and sentiments among intellectuals everywhere in the world, an international community of private persons can be built outside and parallel to the official world structure. It is also not inconceivable that the members of such a community, through sustained and concerted efforts of the imagination and the will, could in time create the conditions out of which the problems of world conflict could be solved by nonviolent and rational means. The activities of international scientists in developing plans and pressing for an international ban on the testing of atomic weapons is a case in point, as is the work of international scientists in the Antarctica Treaty and in the International Geophysical Year.

Having been convinced by the power of the idea that a world college built upon such concepts should somehow be made to exist, several of us joined in the summer of 1963 to conduct an experiment in discovering how it might be brought about. Among the group were Amiya Chakravarty, philosopher from India and a close associate of Tagore and Ghandi in earlier days; Sir Robert Watson-Watt, scientist from Great Britain; and Takeshi Ishida, political scientist from Japan. The experiment took place on a small campus on Long Island, through the cooperation of members of the Society of Friends who had originally formed a committee on a Friends World College.

The plan of action for the experiment was comparatively simple. The existing world organization most capable of enlisting the cooperation of governments in a project of this kind is the United Nations, since in the Communist countries and many others the only access to private persons is through official channels. And if the model we were making was to be in any sense a prototype for future models, the financing would have to be international in character. Twenty-four United Nations countries, including the Soviet Union and the United States, representing a cross-section of the ideological and geographical areas of the world, were therefore invited to select one student each and to finance his attendance at the experiment. The only requirements were that the student, man or woman, graduate or undergraduate, be seriously interested in world affairs, have competence in the use of the English language, and be between the ages of twenty and thirty. A full-scale world college in the future would of course have to deal with the language problem, probably in the manner of the United Nations, with English and French as the working languages and simultaneous translation for others (a translation of the world's literature into all languages would be an essential component of the humanities curriculum), but for our purposes in the experiment English did serve as a world language without nationalist overtones.

Negotiations with the invited countries were carried on for five months, at which point it was decided to select students from four Latin-American countries, Paraguay, Chile, Mexico and Colombia; two European socialist republics, Poland and Rumania; four African countries, Ghana, Nigeria, Uganda, and Ethiopia; four Asian countries, India, Malaya, Indonesia, and Japan (Hong Kong was also included, as representing the United Kingdom), in addition to France, Egypt, Israel, Jamaica, Canada, and the United States. The Soviet Union expressed serious interest in an invitation to send both a student and a faculty member, but arrangements could not be completed in time to include either one in the six-week session. The invitation to Cuba brought no reply, nor did the one to Communist China.

Our hope that it would be possible for all the invited governments to select and finance a student was shown to be overoptimistic. Few governments, including that of the United States, have at this point an allocation of funds for purposes of this kind; the selection and financing of students is carried out in bilateral arrangements between countries. As several of the United Nations and various embassy officials pointed out, the dollar shortage afflicting most countries made it impossible to send students directly from the home country to the world college for the experimental period. Accordingly, with the help of a network of individuals and private organizations in this country and abroad who cooperated with the agencies of the governments, approximately 300 representative students were recommended and a final selection of twenty-four was made, most of them being students already in this country. In each case, the selection was approved by the invited governments. The students were financed by contributions from individuals and foundations in this country.

The resident faculty was joined by Professor Antipa Othieno, an educator from Kenya; and Professor Anthony Pearce, geographer, bibliographer, and professor of government at New York University; and, for a ten-day period, Professor Arthur Lall, former head of the Indian delegation to the Geneva disarmament negotiations and now professor of international relations at Cornell University. Nonresident faculty visited for periods of one to three days from the United Nations secretariat and delegations, and from the embassies of the participating countries. They included Dr. Marion Dobrosielski of Poland, Counsellor to the Polish Embassy and a professor of philosophy at the University of Warsaw; Dr. Ion Moraru of the Rumanian delegation to the United Nations and professor of economics at the University of Bucharest; Taghi Nasr, Director of Economic and Social Affairs at the United Nations and professor of economics at the University of Tehran; and a number of others.

The results of the experiment exceeded our hopes. They showed that although the problems of organization and finance for a full-fledged world college are enormously complicated, the idea itself is not only feasible but is capable of generating a degree of intellectual energy and a quality of understanding in world affairs that none of us had seen in any other kind of institution. The students did in fact become aware of their membership in a world community and became capable of looking at their own culture and its place in world society with a breadth of perspective that surprised even themselves. Before long they began to speak of "our" point of view, by which they meant a world point of view, when referring to international issues. As one of the Asian students, writing at the conclusion of the experiment, put it, "I think in terms more of the wider consequences of a particular event; no longer only of its effects upon me or upon just a scattering of people close to me. A world issue has meaning in space and time." This was particularly noticeable in the conventional situation of ideological conflict between Eastern and Western policies. The presence in the student body of young people who had been born and raised under Communist educational systems meant that the rest of the students were presented with a clear expression of the world as seen by the Communist countries. This was also true in reverse for the Communist students. They listened for the first time, in a completely open situation, to students and scholars educated in a system different from their own.

At the beginning of the experiment, most statements by the Communist students in discussions were polemical, and the vocabulary was studded with phrases about Western imperialists, capitalism, and the military aggressions of the West. It was clear that their education had taught them a dialectical mode of argument in which there were two sides, one of which was always wrong. But the defense and exegesis of a "Western" point of view was not possible in the context of the world-college setting, since there was no clear definition of what the "West" included, and there was such a variety of interpretation by the

173

African, Asian, and Latin-American students of Western and Eastern policies that the simplistic notion of a virtuous noncolonial East and a malignant imperialist West disintegrated under discussion.

When one student asserted firmly that elections in Poland were as free as those in the United States, he was challenged, not by the American student nor by anyone from the West, but by a student from Africa who had studied American voting procedures and whose own country had a one-party system. The challenge was not ideological but factual. One student pointed out that in a world college our purpose was not to argue but to inquire, and that the difference between the college and the world outside was that here political issues were the subject of scholarly analysis and not occasions for propaganda. What was needed in this case, he said, was a brief paper by a competent person on the means of choosing political leadership under Communist states and in the democracies. On another occasion, when the discussion turned on a blanket justification of Communist policy in Latin America, the difference between the operation of European communism in Rumania and party operations in Latin America was explained by a Latin American who had been close to the party in his home country but rejected it because he found that the leadership continually sacrificed the welfare of the peasants for the political advantage to be gained in allying with the military.

The particular genius of the world college was the way in which it purified discussion of the irrelevancies of political hostility. The presence of intelligent, informed, and concerned students and scholars from every part of the world and from nearly every kind of political system meant that all public statements about the world at large were listened to by such a variety of minds that one soon became very careful not to generalize about Africa, the free world, communism, the West, God, or art, without considering carefully the variety of meanings and interpretations the terms could contain.

Ideological conflict in this setting gave way to serious efforts on all sides to understand the problems that produced the conflicts. National and cultural differences did not disappear, Moslems were not converted to Judaism, atheists to Christians, Communists to capitalists, nor did national loyalties disappear. What happened was that the perception of one's own place in a pluralistic system of ideas and values became more precise, and the possibility of a community of interest looking toward the improvement of the common lot of all mankind became clear and real.

As the seminars and discussions continued over the period of the experiment, the national origins of the students became less and less important, and each member of the college community came to consider his colleagues and himself not as official representatives of given cultures but as friends who thought this way or that way about whatever was discussed. Students became interested in how they had come to believe what they professed. Each was asked to write an account of his own education and how it had affected his outlook; the accounts were mimeographed and distributed to the whole college as content for a discussion of world education; two students began a study of the differences and similarities in educational background in relation to the problem of developing an international curriculum that might be introduced to colleges throughout the entire world.

What, then, would be the curriculum of a world college, and how would it differ from any other kind? Obviously, in the short period of the experiment it was not possible to present in advance a full world curriculum in the humanities, the arts, and the social and natural sciences. In any case, our goal was not to present a curriculum already made but to investigate the way to make one, and to develop a content as we went along. To this end, we had as our major resource the knowledge already possessed by the students and scholars of the college itself. The arts were introduced into the curriculum, sometimes by records chosen and played by students or faculty, at other times by recommended readings, films, or performances and demonstrations by students and visitors, and by discussion of what was read, seen, or heard. Since there were no precedents for what we were trying to do, there were no inhibitions on how we did it. Our first appointed task was therefore to discover what a cross-section of well-educated contemporary world youth actually knew, what ideas it valued most, and what were the central issues around which it believed a body of world knowledge should be profitably built.

During the first day of the experiment, each student prepared a statement of the issues in the world that in his judgment were central to the curriculum, the status of the issues, the knowledge about them in his own country, and the contribution he believed he could make to a better understanding of them. The results were immediately mimeographed and distributed to the whole college. They furnished the basis on which the first week's seminars were built. The college met every morning, with all students and faculty members present for a two-hour seminar (it often could not be stopped before three hours) led either by a single member of the faculty or by a symposium of students, or of faculty, or both. Smaller informal seminars were held each afternoon, with students assigned on the basis of their knowledge and their interests, and the faculty serving as tutors to each member of the seminar.

The three major issues that concerned the student body were disarmament and world peace, the ideological conflict between East and West, and the emergence of new countries, including their new educational systems. On the basis of the reports from the students, seminar topics were developed for each week, and individuals from the resident and nonresident faculty and from the student body were called upon to prepare the presentations at the daily seminar, with the director serving as impartial chairman of the discussion that followed each presentation. Students and faculty members aided each other in the preparation of the seminars, and statements were written and bibliographies prepared as a result of the discussion. These, too, were mimeographed and made available to everyone; they became part of the basic source material in the library that was gradually being assembled through loans and purchases.

The seminar topics began immediately to develop an organic unity from day to day and week to week, a unity that depended not so much upon the organized disciplines and subject matter of the conventional curriculum, but upon the continual movement outward from the central issues into those fields of knowledge—sociology, history, religion, philosophy, politics, and psychology—that could help clarify the issues. For example, Professor Chakravarty's discussion of "Some Problems of War and Peace" during the first week led very quickly to a series of further discussions in psychology and philosophy, on the nature of man himself, and to discussions on the difference between African and Indian societies in the way they think about and are taught about war, the socialization of the individual by national habits and customs, the role of science in changing the character of war, and the goals of life as conceived by the Islamic religions in contrast to Communist states. The educational plan was to organize such varying subjects into a form in which they could be dealt with in subject-matter terms during subsequent seminars. Sir Robert Watson-Watt dealt with one cluster of subjects under the topic "The Impact of Science on Contemporary Society." Professor Moraru and Professor Othieno dealt with another set under the topic "Revolution and the Nation-State." Professor Chakravarty considered still another under "Freedom and Independence as a World Concept."

It soon became clear that much of the existing body of knowledge on the topics being considered was irrelevant to a college that wished to consider issues from a world point of view, and that relatively few of the conventional texts used in universities could be useful in achieving the purposes of the experiment. The students, having been trained in their universities to deal with academic topics set for them and to write papers that first summarized the existing literature and then summed up the general conclusions reached by the authorities, found it very difficult to think freshly in their own terms about the issues they had chosen to write about. (Each student decided to write a research paper during the term.) However, they were forced to a new approach by the absence of books and authorities to summarize. With varying success, they learned to search for original sources, to use the ideas and knowledge of their colleagues in the student body and faculty, and to rely for their educational development more on discussion and on tutorial and seminar sessions. Both students and faculty called upon the resources of the major university libraries in the New York City area, after bibliographies were developed by the faculty around topics chosen for further exploration in tutorial sessions. Some of the items were original United Nations documents, others were translations of works from the countries of the students' origin, others were documents prepared by the governments themselves.

One of the most successful demonstrations of the value of the curriculum came during a four-hour session on the status of contemporary China; it may serve as an example of what might be accomplished in a world college of the future. The title of the seminar presentation was "Images of Contemporary China." It was divided into four parts: a brief summary of the major geographic facts in historical perspective by Professor Pearce, followed by statements on the "Indian Image of China" by Professor Chakravarty, the "Japanese Image" by Professor Ishida, and the "Soviet Image" by a student from Poland. Each of the participants was not only well informed on his topic, but two had spent time in China and one in Tibet; consequently they knew the Chinese problems at first hand. Another had been taught in the Soviet Union about Soviet policy in relation to China. And each tried to express as honestly as possible, without national bias, the views of one culture about another culture.

If we had time for an entire year of study of the four cultures represented in the discussion—their literature, art, philosophy, politics, sociology, geography, and history—the educational results would have been deep and lasting. As it was, traces of the single session were to be found in almost every part of the subsequent discussion, since we had hit upon a way of approaching a world issue that united the concerns of the Communists, non-Communists, and nonaligned alike. In fact, the absence of a student or faculty member from Communist China was so keenly felt by all that several students volunteered to prepare material on behalf of the absent member. The China session also created a demand for sessions of a similar kind on the attitude of other cultures to the United States, and several students who had listened to the Marxist analysis of American policy asked explicitly for a full statement by a competent authority on the ideological base of American foreign policy. The political views of the students were varied in the extreme, both in foreign-policy matters and in politics in general, ranging through various kinds of socialism and communism, alignment and nonalignment, parliamentary democracy and one-party government.

In broad terms, it would be accurate to say that this section of world youth was much more critical of the United States than of the Soviet Union or even Communist China. American motives in urging the test ban were held to be an effort to preserve nuclear superiority, while the motive of the other countries was to prevent war. American policy toward China was stagnant and dangerous, while Soviet policy was realistic and sensible. (Briefings on the China-United Nations question by the Soviet and American delegations at the U.N. on a field trip failed, for the most part, to alter these views.)

There were several very interesting results of the barrage of criticism. Perhaps the major effect was the realization that the United States is by far the most fascinating and important force in world affairs, and that the world habit of thinking in terms of a two-power bloc with one side right and the other wrong is an addiction that does harm to the facts. It also became clear that criticism of the United States was much easier to come by than criticism of the Soviet Union and its allies (the college agreed, upon explicit request from some members, not to refer to Poland and Rumania as satellite states but as socialist republics), since there was so much criticism of America by Americans to serve as a model. (Most of those from outside the United States felt themselves to be fully qualified to criticize us since they had already lived here as students. In addition, they had the concept of America given them by our television and motion pictures.)

Another troubling misconception that was difficult for the students to grapple with was the actual diversity of American political opinion within the American system of government. Students would, for example, attack the American government because Senator Goldwater argued against the test-ban treaty, and for a time no amount of reference by others to President Kennedy's speeches and public statements could convince most members of the student body that the United States Government genuinely wanted the test ban. The assumption was usually made that the government could take a liberal policy line if only it wanted to, and there was little understanding of the link between public policy and the voting power of the electorate. No matter at what point discussions of foreign policy began, they usually ended in a discussion of American policy. Although this was in one sense flattering to America and its place in world affairs, it often distorted the issues themselves. What saved the situation intellectually was the fact that, owing to the college context, it was impossible to view America in anything but a world perspective. The faculty was not American and, by virtue of its scholarly objectivity, remained consistently nonaligned. The one American student was both quiet and in some ways more critical of America than the other students. Thus, in the absence of American defense against criticism, the critics made their wildest statements, as it were, into the open air.

The assumption was made almost universally at the beginning that America was responsible for the problems of the world, in having created them, and was therefore responsible for cleaning them up. The way to clean them up was to accede to the demands of the critics for changes in policy. The foreign aid program was taken for granted rather than valued as a twentieth-century departure by the United States from the norm of nationalist economic exploitation, and it was generally assumed that the foreign aid, being mostly military in character, was simply a means of buying military alliances. It was also assumed, without question, that this richest of countries was automatically responsible for the poor ones and that the poorer countries had a perfect right to expect financial aid, without strings.

As the study of world affairs continued, and research topics were chosen by the students in consultation with their tutors, the clichés of world thought began to disappear in favor of analysis in depth of the multi-sided and complicated nature of the issues. One research paper on the Negro and James Baldwin by a European student, which began as an exposure of the evils of the American treatment of the Negro, developed, as the sessions went on, into a paper on social imagery, using the thesis of Baldwin's *Nobody Knows My Name* as a theme for illustrating the difficulty of accurate social perception of the reality of cultural differences. The fact that the writer was a Communist made the enlargement of understanding even more gratifying.

The implications of the experiment for future programs of world education and for eventual development of a world university or universities are striking. There was no doubt in the mind of anyone in the student body or faculty that something quite remarkable had happened during the short life of the college. Visible progress had been made in developing a new kind of curriculum in the arts and sciences. The individual research papers, which ranged from the analysis of the politics and ethics of nonalignment to the description and appraisal of three international universities (Tagore's Santiniketan, Moscow's Friendship University, and the Experimental College in Copenhagen) were in themselves a contribution to the content of a new curriculum. Each student learned to know and to understand in some measure the cultural values and individual virtues of societies other than his own. The hope of the faculty that students could be taught to look at the world from the perspective of world citizenship was in large part realized.

Were the East-West Center in Hawaii to be expanded conceptually to include students and scholars from everywhere in the West and East, Communist and non-Communist alike, and from all seven continents, rather than acting as an American link to Asia, it would approach the new concepts reached by the World College experiment. If Friendship University in Moscow were expanded in concept to include non-Communist Western and Eastern students, faculty, and curriculum, rather than serving as a training center for Soviet technology, it would become a world university.

In other words, we learned how it could be done and what it would mean if it were done. Aside from anything else, the experiment produced a wealth of ideas for developing within American institutions of higher education programs of study and research by foreign students that would not only enrich the American curriculum but would greatly increase the dimension of world understanding of both Americans and foreign students alike. To call upon the resources of students from abroad in constructing inner communities of world citizens within the larger framework of the American student body would provide a series of models not unlike the one we constructed on Long Island. It would also help to avoid that particular kind of dislocation which occurs when foreign students come to the United States and are educated into a trained incapacity to readapt to the conditions of their home country.

In summary, I think it is fair to say that the experiment demonstrated not only that a world college is possible, but that one direct way toward that possibility lies in building world communities within national boundaries as forerunners of the day when a world community can be developed on a world scale. The point received dramatic illustration on the last day of the college. As one can imagine, by the end of the session we had become a community of persons bound together by friendships, common interests, and a genuine sense of unity. Into that community, on the final day, came a group of ten young Negroes who were active as members of the Student Nonviolent Coordinating Committee in Georgia, Virginia, Alabama, and Mississippi; they were on a brief ten-day vacation from jails, beatings, and demonstrations.

After the visitors swam with the World College students (there were helter-skelter relay races organized between the Communists and the Western nations), the young Southerners joined us for the final seminar. Each of them spoke briefly, in a quiet way, describing his jail life, his experience with police brutality, and his reasons for joining the movement. Then their young leader described the philosophy of nonviolence. Immediately the World College students joined in discussion. Some of them had also been in jail, others had seen oppression by their governments. They spoke of the strategy of freedom, revolution, protest movements, and totalitarianism. Some attacked the philosophy of nonviolence and advocated stronger measures. The American visitors then patiently explained why they loved their country, what democracy meant to them, and why they wished to find a way, through sacrifice, by which democracy could be made to work on a world scale. At the close of the seminar, the young Negroes invited us to join them in singing "We Shall Overcome." As the wide circle of young people from everywhere in the world, white and black, Asian and African, Western and Eastern, stood side by side with their teachers and their new American friends, singing "We shall make a new world," in a world's variety of voices and accents, all trace of cynicism, skepticism, and even self-consciousness vanished. At that moment, each knew in his bones that to make a new world was possible.

NOTES/BIBLIOGRAPHY

NOTES

The abbreviations in the notes are the code numbers supplied
by the library of the League of Nations at the Palais des Nations
in Geneva and by the archives of UNESCO in Paris.
See Bibliography.

1

THE NEED FOR A WORLD UNIVERSITY

1. C.445, M.165, 1925, XII, pp. 26–30.
2. *Ibid.*, p. 27.
3. Alexander Marc, "Mission of an International University,"
   International Social Science Bulletin of UNESCO, IV
   (Spring, 1952), 227.
4. *A United Nations University*, third draft (Ann Arbor,
   Mich., 1962), Sect. III, p. 7.
5. Marc, *op. cit.*, 229.
6. Eugene Staley, "A Proposal for a United Nations University" (Unpublished, Menlo Park, Cal., 1960), p. 1.

7. *A United Nations University*, Sect. II, p. 5.
8. Staley, *op. cit.*, p. 1.
9. Marc, *op. cit.*, 228.
10. *Proceedings of the First Biennial Conference of the World Federation of Education Associations* (Edinburgh, 1925), pp. 412–21.
11. *Ibid.*, p. 413.
12. T. S. Simey and F. T. H. Fletcher, "Report on an International Institute of the Social Sciences," *International Social Science Bulletin of UNESCO*, III (Autumn, 1951), 636.
13. Paul Otlet, *L'Université Internationale*, Indice No. 378 (Brussels, 1920), p. 12.
14. UNESCO/prep.com./42.
15. Marc, *op. cit.*, 226.
16. C.3, M.3, 1924, XII, p. 46.
17. *Ibid.*, p. 42.
18. ECO/conf./9, p. 70.
19. Sem.Sec./1/13, p. 1.
20. *A United Nations University*, Foreword.

2

THE DEVELOPED ALTERNATIVES TO A WORLD UNIVERSITY

1. Fletcher School catalogue, 1963–64, p. 14.
2. Egypt, Pakistan, Japan, Thailand, India, South Korea, Switzerland, Liberia, Nigeria, Canada, England, Norway, Jordan, Federal Republic of Germany.
3. Fletcher School catalogue, p. 48. Italics mine.
4. *Ibid.*, p. 41; similar references p. 44 (Diplomacy 8A) and p. 39 (Politics 753).
5. *Ibid.*, p. 15.
6. WS/048.28, p. 6.
7. Elton B. McNeil, "An International University," *Bulletin of the Atomic Scientists*, XVIII (October, 1962), 24.
8. A discussion of the Graduate Institute of International Studies in Geneva, probably the closest contender, is found in Chapter 5.

3

HISTORY OF THE IDEA OF WORLD EDUCATION

1. A detailed discussion of the Brussels experiment begins Chapter 5.
2. C.L.13, 1921.
3. C.711, M.423, 1922, XII, p. 26.
4. *Ibid.*
5. C.570, M.224, 1923, XII, pp. 69–71.
6. *Ibid.*, p. 69.
7. *Ibid.*, p. 70.
8. A.96(1), 1923, XII, p. 2.
9. C.3, M.3, 1924, XII, p. 42.
10. *Ibid.*, p. 46.
11. *Ibid.*, pp. 46–47.
12. *Ibid.*, pp. 40–41.
13. *Ibid.*, p. 44.
14. C.I.C.I./R.I./22.
15. *Ibid.*, p. 52.
16. Paul Otlet, *L'Université Internationale*, Indice No. 378 (Brussels, 1920), p. 78.
17. C.I.C.I./R.I./22, p. 6.
18. C.I.C.I./R.I./24.
19. A.31, 1924, XII, p. 31.
20. *Ibid.*, p. 14.
21. C.445, M.165, 1925, XII, pp. 26–30.
22. *Ibid.*, p. 9.
23. *Bulletin of the International University Information Office*, 3, pp. 101 ff.

4

PROPOSALS TO INTERNATIONAL BODIES

1. ECO/conf./9, p. 70; also, UNESCO/prep.com./42.
2. The author's search into UNESCO archives failed to reveal many of the proposals alluded to in official records. It is his understanding that any proposal which was more than a

simple statement of desire would have been included in the official documentation, so the material in this chapter covers essentially all of the proposals discussed at UNESCO. According to Willem Welling of the UNESCO Department of Education, letters favorable to a world university had been received by the Department from Professor Gordon Allport; Advisory Committee, Department of Extramural Studies, University of London; Charles University, Prague; and the Chinese, Mexican, Iranian, and United States delegations to UNESCO. These were simply lodged at UNESCO and have elicited no response further than acknowledgment of receipt. Other private proposals of more substance are discussed in Chapter 5.

3. UNESCO/prep.com./42.
4. UNESCO/prep.com./educ.com./1.
5. UNESCO/prep.com./educ.com./1(a).
6. UNESCO/C/2.
7. *Ibid.*, p. 151.
8. *Records*, General Conference, first session, p. 155.
9. UNESCO/C/prog.com./S.C.educ./8, p. 4.
10. *Ibid.*, p. 5.
11. UNESCO/stud.meeting/4, p. 5.
12. E/233.
13. E/620.
14. E/1694.
15. Sem.Sec./I/13, p. 1.
16. DG/124; see, also, *International Social Science Bulletin of UNESCO*, III (Autumn, 1951), 641–44.
17. *International Social Science Bulletin of UNESCO*, III (Autumn, 1951), 645–55.
18. UNESCO/C/2, p. 33. Italics mine.
19. *Ibid.*, p. 110.

5

SOME PROJECTS AND EXPERIMENTS

1. Paul Otlet, *L'Université Internationale*, Indice No. 378 (Brussels, 1920), pp. 21–27.

2. England, Belgium, Spain, United States, France, Holland, Japan, Mexico, Poland, Switzerland.

3. Otlet, *op. cit.*, p. 78.

4. Alexander Marc, "Mission of an International University," *International Social Science Bulletin of UNESCO*, IV (Spring, 1952), 228.

5. *Proceedings of the First Biennial Conference of the World Federation of Education Associations* (Edinburgh, 1925), pp. 412–24.

6. T. S. Simey and F. T. H. Fletcher, "Report on an International Institute of the Social Sciences," *International Social Science Bulletin of UNESCO*, III (Autumn, 1951), 636.

7. *Ibid.*, 637.

8. *Ibid.*, 638.

9. Max Bedrosian and Paul Obler, "United Nations University Centers: A Proposal to Extend International Understanding Through Education" (Unpublished, Newark, N. J.), p. 1.

10. Eugene Staley, "A Proposal for a United Nations University" (Unpublished, Menlo Park, Cal.), p. 3.

11. See, for example, Henri Laugier, "Pour une Université Internationale des Pays Sous-Développés," *Bulletin of the International Association of Universities*, VIII, 3 (1960).

12. See unpublished "IUA Newsletter," Nos. 1–7 and the unpublished "Report to the Third Weekend Conference on October 21, 1961, on Comments from Leaders on the Akrawi Paper" for a complete presentation of responses.

13. *A United Nations University*, third draft (Ann Arbor, Mich., 1962).

14. Werner Wiskari, "Eisenhower Urges World School," *New York Times*, August 1, 1962, 1.

15. Canada, Jamaica, United States, Chile, Colombia, Mexico, Paraguay, France (2), Netherlands, Israel, United Arab Republic, Hongkong, India, Indonesia, Japan, Malaya, Ethiopia, Ghana, Nigeria, Uganda, Poland, Rumania.

16. An article by Harold Taylor describing the experiment was published in the *Saturday Review* and is reprinted as Appendix D of this book.

BIBLIOGRAPHY

BOOKS AND ARTICLES

Bartlett, Stephen W. "A Dialogue Between Cultures." *Saturday Review*, xlvii (July 18, 1964), 44–47.

Chaturvedi, H. *Tagore at Shantiniketan: A Survey of Dr. Rabindranath Tagore's Educational Experiment at Shantiniketan.* Mathais' Publication, 1934.

Commager, Henry Steele. "Commager Urges World Colleges." *New York Times*, May 13, 1959, 15.

Education and International Life: The Yearbook of Education 1964, ed. George Z. F. Bereday and Joseph A. Lauwerys. New York, Harcourt, Brace and World, 1964.

Elvin, H. L. *Nationalism and Internationalism in Education* (Foundation Oration). Goldsmith's College, London, 1959.

Federation of American Scientists Committee for a United Nations University. "The Need for a U.N. University." *Bulletin of the Atomic Scientists*, xvii (March, 1961), 111–13.

Fields, Robert. "World University in the Making." *The Student*, vIII (May, 1964), 26–27. (Published by COSEC, the Coordinating Secretariat of National Unions of Students.)

Kilpatrick, William Heard. "Creation of World University Advocated as Peace Center." *New York Times*, August 28, 1962, 30.

Laugier, Henri, "Pour une Université Internationale des Pays Sous-Développés." *Bulletin of the International Association of Universities*, vIII, 3 (1960), 202–4.

McNeil, Elton B. "An International University." *Bulletin of the Atomic Scientists*, xvIII (October, 1962), 23–24.

Marc, Alexander. "Mission of an International University." *International Social Science Bulletin of UNESCO*, IV (Spring, 1952), 225–29.

"Netherlands International School." *Times Educational Supplement* (London), 2561 (June 19, 1964), 1689.

Otlet, Paul. Address to World Federation of Education Associations. *Proceedings of the First Biennial Conference of the World Federation of Education Associations*. Edinburgh, 1925.

———. *L'Université Internationale*, Indice No. 378. Brussels, 1920.

Perlmutter, Oscar William. "Foreign, International and Supranational Education." *American Review: A Quarterly of American Affairs* (Bologna, Italy), III (Autumn, 1963), 69–91.

Rabinowitch, Eugene. "Pugwash-Coswa: International Conversations." *Bulletin of the Atomic Scientists*, xIx (June, 1963), 7–12.

Russell, Bertrand. "Proposals for an International University." *The Fortnightly*, cLII (July, 1942), 8–16.

Salam, Abdus. "A New Center for Physics." *Bulletin of the Atomic Scientists*, xxI (December, 1965), 43–45.

Simey, T. S. and F. T. H. Fletcher. "Report on an International Institute of the Social Sciences." *International Social Science Bulletin of UNESCO*, III (Autumn, 1951), 634–41.

Staley, Eugene. "A Proposal for a United Nations University."

V.O.C. Journal of Education (Tuticorn, India), II (August, 1962), 12–18.

Stoker, Spencer. *The Schools and International Understanding.* Chapel Hill, University of North Carolina Press, 1933.

Strømnes, Martin. *World Education for Peace: A Proposal for Special Leading Centers in World Education.* Oslo, Oslo University Press, 1959. (Regionally distributed by UNESCO.)

Taylor, Harold. "The Idea of a World College." *Phi Delta Kappan,* XLIV (June, 1963), 399–402.

———. "The Idea of a World College." *Saturday Review,* XLVII (November 14, 1964), 29–32.

UNESCO, Department of Social Science. "The Proposed Establishment of an International Social Science Center." *International Social Science Bulletin of UNESCO,* III (Autumn, 1951), 644–55.

Wiskari, Werner. "Eisenhower Urges World School." *New York Times,* August 1, 1962, 1.

PUBLIC DOCUMENTS

These are presented chronologically in the form listed by the library of the League of Nations in Geneva and by the archives of UNESCO in Paris.

League of Nations

C.L.13, 1921. Letter of the Secretary-General of the League of Nations.

C.711, M.423, 1922, XII. Committee on Intellectual Co-operation (CIC), minutes of first session.

C.570, M.224, 1923, XII CIC, minutes of second session, including D. N. Bannerjea, "A Proposal for the Establishment of an International University."

A.96(1), 1923, XII.

C.3, M.3, 1924, XII. CIC, minutes of third session.

C.I.C.I./R.I./22. Preliminary report by O. deHalecki (French only), March, 1924.

C.I.C.I./R.I./24. April, 1924.

A.31, 1924, xii. CIC, minutes of third and fourth sessions.

C.445, M.165, 1925, xii. CIC, minutes of sixth session, including R. Barany, "Scheme for the Establishment of an International University."

ECOSOC

E/233. Resolution 22 (iii), October, 1946.

E/620. Rapport du Secrétaire Général sur le Problème de la Création des Laboratoires de Recherche des Nations Unies, January, 1948.

E/858. A French proposal.

E/1694. Report of the Committee of Scientific Experts on the International Research Laboratories, 1950.

E/2590. UNESCO report to ECOSOC, 1953–1954.

E/2735. 1954–1955.

E/2867. 1955–1956.

E/2974. 1956–1957.

UNESCO

ECO/conf./9, November, 1945.

ECO/conf./17.

UNESCO/prep.com./42, May, 1946.

UNESCO/prep.com./educ.com./1, May, 1946. Memorandum on UNESCO education program.

UNESCO/prep.com./educ.com./1(a), May, 1946.

UNESCO/C/2, September, 1946. Report on the program of UNESCO.

UNESCO/C/prog.com./S.C.educ./2, November, 1946.

UNESCO/C/prog.com./S.C.educ./7, December, 1946.

UNESCO/C/prog.com./S.C.educ./8.

Publications, General Conference, first session, December, 1946. Project for a UNESCO Educational Center.

Records, General Conference, first session, 1946.

Sem.Sec./I/13, August, 1947. Seminar on Education for the Development of International Understanding.

UNESCO/stud.meeting/4, February, 1949. Brief Outline of the World University Idea During the Past Thirty Years.

DG/124, April, 1951. Address by J. T. Bodet to a meeting of experts on the question of international social science institutes.

UNESCO/ED/127, June, 1953. Introduction to the Associated Schools Project in Education for International Understanding and Cooperation.

UNESCO/ED/141. Report on activities in 1954.

UNESCO/ED/149. Interim report, activities in 1955 and 1956.

WS/048.28, April, 1958. Some General Observations on Research and Evaluation.

EDPLAN/801/4, 1962. Institut International de Planification de l'Enseignement, Projet de Statut.

INDEX

INDEX

Akrami, Matta, 102
Ali Abadi, Ahmad, 104
American Psychological Institute: proposal to United Nations, 62–63
Angell, Robert, 66, 67, 87
Association for Commitment to World Responsibility: on the tasks of an international university, 5, 6, 11, 12, 14; supported by United States National Student Association, 41–42; proposal, 105–8; supported by Andrew Rice, 108
Austria: League of Nations, 37

Bannerjea, D. N.: proposal to League of Nations, 33–35, 40
Barany, R.: proposal to League of Nations, 4, 46–52
Bedrosian, Max: proposal for United Nations University Centers, 97–98
Bodet, Jaime Torres: proposal to UNESCO while Director General, 65–66
Boulding, Kenneth: on the tasks of an international university, 15
Bowles, Chester, 104

Brussels International University: early opposition to, 40; supported by International Confederation of Students, 41; statute, 74–78; financial difficulties, 79–80; relations with national universities, 81; mentioned, 9, 32
Burckhardt, Carl, 92

Castillejo, J.: amplification of Spanish proposal to League of Nations, 42–44
CERN, 27, 67, 68, 123
Chakravarty, Amiya, 111
China: proposal to UNESCO, 11–12, 58
Chi-Pao, Cheng, 104
Colombia: proposal to UNESCO, 14, 53–54, 55
Committee for a United Nations University: response, 92, 119; proposal, 94–97
Committee for the Promotion of an International University in America: proposal, 102–5; reactions, 104; influence on Association for Commitment to World Responsibility, 105–7 *passim*
Committee on a Friends World

College. *See* Friends World College

Cousins, Norman, 104

Curriculum: limitations of national universities, 22–24, 63–64, 67–68, 89–90. *See also* World University

Czechoslovakia: proposal to League of Nations, 37

deHalecki, O.: evaluation of international universities presented to League of Nations, 37–42

deReynold, G., 32–33, 50–52

Destree, J., 32–33, 50–52

DeVries, E., 94

ECOSOC: consideration of international research centers, 62

Eisenhower, Dwight: proposes international school, 109

Ewerts, Karl J. *See* International University Foundation

Exchange programs: limitations of, 20, 21

Federation of American Scientists: influence on Association for Commitment to World Responsibility, 105–7 *passim*. *See also* Committee for a United Nations University

Fleischman, Theodore, 88

Fletcher, F. T. H. *See* International Association of University Professors and Lecturers

Fletcher School of Law and Diplomacy: curriculum limitations, 22–23

Ford Foundation, 80

Freymond, Jacques, 104

Friends World College: committee on, 60; pilot project, 109–12; reactions, 111–13

Geneva, University of, 83, 84

Graduate Institute of International Studies: limitations, 85–88; mentioned, 83–88, 100, 104, 121–22

Graham, Frank, 104

Greece: proposal to League of Nations, 13–14, 36–37, 40, 54

Huber, Max, 92

International Academic Associations: functions and limitations, 26–27

International Association of University Professors and Lecturers: proposal for a world university, 9–10, 89–92

International Confederation of Students: support of Brussels International University, 41; mentioned, 74

International Labor Organization, 84

International Radio University, 88–89, 93

International Social Science Institute, 61

International Social Science Research Center, 66–67

International Society for the Establishment of a World University: proposal for a world university, 92–93; pilot project, 94

International University Foundation: proposal, 98–99

International University Information Office, 37, 117

Ishida, Takeshi, 111

Jaramillo-Arango, Jaime, 53

Javits, Senator Jacob, 102

Jewish University of Jerusalem, 82

Kilpatrick, William Heard, 102, 105

LaFontaine, Henri, 32, 73

Lall, Arthur, 111

Laugier, Henri: proposals for an international university, 101–2; mentioned, 62, 63

League of Nations: proposals presented to, 4, 13–14, 33–37, 46–50; support of Brussels International University, 31–32; Committee on Intellectual Cooperation, 32–33, 35–37, 45–46, 50–52; reactions to proposals for world university, 32–33, 116–18; formal resolution of proposals for a world university, 45–46,